Understanding

Johnny Tremain

New and future titles in the Understanding Great Literature series include:

Understanding

Johnny Tremain

UNDERSTANDING GREAT LITERATURE

Elizabeth Weiss Vollstadt

Lucent Books
P.O. Box 289011
San Diego, CA 92198-9011

On Cover: American Revolutionary war soldiers.

Library of Congress Cataloging-in-Publication Data

Vollstadt, Elizabeth Weiss, 1942–
  Understanding Johnny Tremain / by Elizabeth Weiss Vollstadt.
    p. cm. — (Understanding great literature)
  Includes bibliographical references and index.
  Summary: Discusses the young adult book "Johnny Tremain" by
  Esther Forbes, including the author's life, and the book's plot,
  characters, and theme.
    ISBN 1-56006-849-3
  1. Forbes, Esther. Johnny Tremain. 2. Boston (Mass.)—History—
  Revolution, 1775–1783—Literature and the revolution. 3.
  United States—History—Revolution, 1775–1783—Literature
  and the revolution. 4. Historical fiction, American—History and
  criticism. 5. Children's stories, American—History and criticism.
  I. Title II. Series.
    PS3511 .O3495 J6538 2001
    813'.54—dc21   00-011641

Printed in the U.S.A.

Contents

FOREWORD

"**E**xcept for a living man, there is nothing more wonderful than a book!" wrote the widely respected nineteenth-century teacher and writer Charles Kingsley. A book, he continued, "is a message to us from human souls we never saw. And yet these [books] arouse us, terrify us, teach us, comfort us, open our hearts to us as brothers." There are many different kinds of books, of course; and Kingsley was referring mainly to those containing literature—novels, plays, short stories, poems, and so on. In particular, he had in mind those works of literature that were and remain widely popular with readers of all ages and from many walks of life.

Such popularity might be based on one or several factors. On the one hand, a book might be read and studied by people in generation after generation because it is a literary classic, with characters and themes of universal relevance and appeal. Homer's epic poems, the *Iliad* and the *Odyssey*, Chaucer's *Canterbury Tales*, Shakespeare's *Hamlet* and *Romeo and Juliet*, and Dickens's *A Christmas Carol* fall into this category. Some popular books, on the other hand, are more controversial. Mark Twain's *Huckleberry Finn* and J. D. Salinger's *The Catcher in the Rye*, for instance, have their legions of devoted fans who see them as great literature; while others view them as less than worthy because of their racial depictions, profanity, or other factors.

Still another category of popular literature includes realistic modern fiction, including novels such as Robert Cormier's *I Am the Cheese* and S. E. Hinton's *The Outsiders*. Their keen social insights and sharp character portrayals have consistently reached out to and captured the imaginations of many teenagers and young adults; and for this reason they are often assigned and studied in schools.

These and other similar works have become the "old standards" of the literary scene. They are the ones that people most often read, discuss, and study; and each has, by virtue of its content, critical success, or just plain longevity, earned the right to be the subject of a book examining its content. (Some, of course, like the *Iliad* and *Hamlet*, have been the subjects of numerous books already; but their literary stature is so lofty that there can never be too many books about them!) For millions of readers and students in one generation after another, each of these works becomes, in a sense, an adventure in appreciation, enjoyment, and learning.

The main purpose of Lucent's Understanding Great Literature series is to aid the reader in that ongoing literary adventure. Each volume in the series focuses on a single literary work that a majority of critics and teachers view as a classic and/or that is widely studied and discussed in schools. A typical volume first tells why the work in question is important. Then follow detailed overviews of the author's life, the work's historical background, its plot, its characters, and its themes. Numerous quotes from the work, as well as by critics and other experts, are interspersed throughout and carefully documented with footnotes for those who wish to pursue further research. Also included is a list of ideas for essays and other student projects relating to the work, an appendix of literary criticisms and analyses by noted scholars, and a comprehensive annotated bibliography.

The great nineteenth-century American poet Henry David Thoreau once quipped: "Read the best books first, or you may not have a chance to read them at all." For those who are reading or about to read the "best books" in the literary canon, the comprehensive, thorough, and thoughtful volumes of the Understanding Great Literature series are indispensable guides and sources of enrichment.

"That a Man Can Stand Up"

> "It is all so much simpler than you think. . . . We give all we have, lives, property, safety, skills . . . we fight, we die, for a simple thing. Only that a man can stand up."

James Otis speaks these words at a gathering of Patriot leaders in Esther Forbes's historical novel *Johnny Tremain*, as they prepare for the possibility of war against Britain. They are stirring words to the novel's title character, young Johnny Tremain. A silversmith apprentice in pre-Revolutionary Boston, Johnny becomes a staunch Patriot, embroiled in the political turmoil of his day.

They were no less stirring words to the young people who first read *Johnny Tremain*. The book was published in 1943, when the United States was in the middle of World War II, and feelings of patriotism were high. Men and women by the thousands were fighting to free the world from the oppression of Nazism and fascism. Their younger brothers and sisters at home were doing what they could to help the war effort. Like Johnny, they believed that some ideals were worth fighting for and even dying for.

In the more than fifty years since the publication of *Johnny Tremain*, much has happened to make young people more skeptical of government—the turmoil of the 1960s, the unpopular Vietnam War, the Watergate scandal, and more recently, the scandals associated with the Clinton administration. As a result, today's teenagers are less blindly patriotic than the World War II generation and less likely to risk their lives for a cause that may or may not be just.

Yet some things have not changed since *Johnny Tremain* first appeared. Young people still look for causes to believe in, ideals to give meaning to their lives. They still face inner conflicts as they move from childhood to adulthood. They still worry about the future. They still enjoy reading about young people in different times. And they still love an exciting story.

A Landmark of Historical Fiction

Johnny Tremain offers all of that. It has been called "a landmark of historical fiction for children,"[1] and praised for its author's skill in bringing pre-Revolutionary Boston to life. The year after its

Johnny Tremain *has received glowing reviews for its stunningly accurate portrayal of pre-Revolutionary life in Boston.*

publication, 1944, it received the prestigious Newbery Award as "the most distinguished contribution to American literature for children."[2] That same year, an article in *Horn Book*, a well respected journal of children's literature, noted:

> *Johnny Tremain* may well be counted the first classic story of Boston for young people. This is not alone because of the accurate picture of the pre-Revolutionary town, with its wandering streets and busy wharves, its crafts and trades, markets and merchants, nor because of the rich abundance of details about the manners of the period, its way of living and customs of trade, nor even because it is an arresting portrayal of the stubborn resistance of the Patriots and townspeople against arbitrary acts of the British Parliament. It is a distinguished book, primarily, because the people in it are vigorously endowed with the human quality which binds one generation to another.[3]

Johnny himself is a character whose contradictions can be found in teenagers in any time and place. At the beginning of the book he is fourteen years old, a talented silversmith apprentice in the Lapham household, and responsible for keeping his master's business alive. He knows he is talented, and he bullies and scolds the other two apprentices. He is arrogant, opinionated, and self-centered. But he is also kind to his master's youngest grandchildren, Cilla, his own age, and Isannah, just eight years old. And he turns down an opportunity to apprentice with Paul Revere because he knows the Laphams depend on him. Then tragedy strikes in the form of an accident that cripples his right hand. Without the manual dexterity to be a silversmith, Johnny must find a new direction. During the two years that the book covers, he finds new friendships and ideals, and also faces more tragedy. Like most teens in any time, he is often confused by the contradictions he sees in the world around him.

Also like many teens, he takes his special relationship with a young girl, in his case Cilla, for granted until he faces competition from other young men. As one reviewer wrote, "Johnny suffers and doubts, grouches and *grows*,"[4] and in the end becomes a man.

Life Long Ago

Johnny's life also offers insights into the life of a teenager who lived 225 years ago. Forbes carefully researched the details of apprentices' lives through diaries and other firsthand accounts to make his life authentic. Orphaned at thirteen, he was expected to earn his keep as an apprentice. Work was hard and long—six days a week. Formal schooling was not an option. Johnny could read and write thanks to his mother, who taught him herself. When his hand was crippled, no social service agencies existed to help him. Mr. Lapham might be kind and not turn him out, but at age fourteen, he had to find other work for himself. If he didn't, with his quick tongue and cockiness ever likely to get him into trouble, he could well "end up on the gallows,"[5] as Mrs. Lapham predicts. One critic has stated that Johnny is so real that readers sometimes go to Boston expecting to find his mother's grave in the cemetery.

Readers of Johnny Tremain *quickly become immersed in history as Johnny witnesses and sometimes participates in the events around him, such as the Boston Tea Party.*

Also vividly described is the American Revolution. The reader is with Johnny at the Boston Tea Party ("The axes went through the wood easily enough—the canvas [wrapping the tea] made endless trouble. Johnny had never worked so hard in his life.") The reader is there too when Johnny sees British reinforcements preparing to march to Lexington on April 19 ("The narrow course of Tremont Street was filled to the brim and overflowing with the waiting scarlet-coated men. Like a river of blood.").[6] As one critic wrote for *Horn Book* in 1962, Johnny's involvement in the Revolution is so much a part of the plot that "reading about Johnny Tremain becomes reading about the American Revolution. If any book can be called a prototype of all that historical fiction should be, this book merits that appellation."[7]

Thus *Johnny Tremain* remains an important book for several reasons. It presents a moving story of a young boy's growth to manhood in a turbulent time of history. Even more significant, however, is that as he grows, Johnny struggles with great ideas— human rights and the value of the individual, or the "rights of man" as they are referred to in the book. The world is vastly different today from pre-Revolutionary Boston and from the days of World War II, yet the United States still struggles with the ideals of human rights and the problems caused by discrimination in many forms. Young people today are still challenged with making their country a place where "a man can stand up."

CHAPTER ONE

Esther Forbes: Steeped in Colonial History

W riting about the colonial period in America was natural for Esther Forbes, the author of *Johnny Tremain*. She was born on June 28, 1891, in Westboro, Massachusetts, a small town west of Boston, and moved to nearby Worcester when she was seven. Among her ancestors were Revolutionary War leader Sam Adams and a young woman who died in a Cambridge jail in the 1600s awaiting trial as a witch.

"I was brought up on stories of early New England," she once said, giving an example. "Far back, two uncles of my father had been captured by Indians as little boys. They lived to be powerful chiefs among the Canadian tribes. As old men, they came back to their father's farm in Westboro. They knew no English and could remember little except the brook where they used to play."[8]

Both of Esther's parents were well educated. Her father, William Forbes, graduated from Amherst College in Massachusetts in 1871 and traveled to Constantinople (now Istanbul), Turkey, to teach math at Robert College. While there, he saw the archaeological excavation of ancient Troy and brought back stories that later fueled his young daughter's imagination. Returning home, he became a lawyer in Westboro, and in 1888, three years before Esther's birth, was appointed judge of the probate court in Worcester.

Her mother, Harriette Merrifield Forbes, attended Oread Academy in Worcester, one of the earliest educational institutions for women. A respected historian, she would eventually publish several reference books, including *New England Diaries, 1602–1800* in 1923 and *Gravestones of Early New England and the Men Who Made Them, 1653–1800* in 1927. She would also work with her daughter as she researched colonial history.

An Early Storyteller

Esther Forbes was the fifth of six children, although her younger brother did not survive infancy. It was a busy family of high achievers. The four older children were excellent students and went on to prestigious universities. Esther, however, was different. From the time she was a very small child, she liked to tell stories and would entertain her sister Katharine, who shared a room with her. When she was eight years old, she joined her older siblings and two friends in publishing a neighborhood magazine. Her first published writing appeared in the second issue, an article about the Wayside Inn in Sudbury, Massachusetts.

When she was nine years old, Esther fell ill with rheumatic fever, a severe infectious disease that usually strikes children and often causes serious damage to the heart. (Today, rheumatic fever is much less com-

Esther Forbes was born and raised not far from Boston, the setting of Johnny Tremain.

mon, as it is caused by a strep infection that can now be treated early with antibiotics.) Esther was left with a damaged heart that would remain a problem throughout her life. During the long weeks in bed, her mother encouraged her to read, write, draw, and paint.

At the age of twelve, Esther started writing her first novel, titled *Patroclus*. It was about the Greek hero Achilles and the fall of Troy. "An industrious little beaver, I always had a novel going after that," she said in a *New York Times Book Review* interview. "I read Caesar, and the Gallic Wars became a novel. There was another about Rome at the time of the Renaissance. Probably there were five or six altogether. Naturally I never rewrote, but would go along until I got dissatisfied and then quit to start another."[9] Not until years later did it occur to her to write about places and time periods closer to home.

Indifferent Student, Superior Writer

Despite her creativity and intelligence, Esther was not a good student like her older siblings. She found it hard to pay attention, and one teacher described her spelling as "poor . . . bad . . . and atrocious."[10] It is now believed that some of these problems were probably caused by Forbes's eyesight—she was very nearsighted—and by some form of dyslexia. Her spelling and grammar remained bad throughout her entire life.

Nevertheless, her writing itself was apparently superior, and a grammar school teacher once lectured her about plagiarism. Mrs. Forbes was quick to defend her daughter, assuring the teacher that Esther had, indeed, written the composition in question.

After graduating from high school, Esther took classes at the Worcester Art Museum and Boston University. From 1909 to 1912, she attended Bradford Academy, a junior college in Bradford, Massachusetts. While her teachers were constantly critical of her handwriting and spelling, they knew her papers were special and sometimes questioned her authorship. But Esther kept her "serious writing"—her own short stories—to herself.

Her biographer Margaret Erskine, the wife of Esther's nephew, writes:

> If she was "really crazy to write," as she put it, she would put off her school work, take a walk in the country to work out the plot of a short story, get back and write it down in a few hours, "which only meant failing in all my classes one day or perhaps two or three. Not enough to get me in serious trouble."[11]

Wisconsin Years

Esther Forbes graduated from Bradford in 1912 and returned home. She took part in the family's busy social life and traveled to Boston to take writing courses. Then in 1915, her sister Katharine took a teaching job at the University of Wisconsin. Forbes went along to take courses at the university. She continued to write, and in 1916, her love of horses and riding produced an award-winning story, "Break-Neck Hill." Her instructor at Wisconsin wrote, "This is one of the best undergraduate stories I have read in a long time. The matter is fresh and interesting and the style has movement and character. . . . It is full of striking detail."[12] The story was published in the November 1916 issue of the *Wisconsin Literary Magazine* and was included in the *O. Henry Memorial Award Prize Stories of 1920.*

When the United States entered World War I in 1917, a call went out for volunteers to replace farmworkers who were serving overseas in the army. Forbes volunteered and was sent to a farm in West Virginia. Noting her skill with horses, the farmer gave her the job of driving the farm's team of horses. "One of the proudest moments of my life," she later said, "was when the farmer appointed me as a teamster to work only with horses, instead of merely shucking corn and picking apples like the other girls."[13] She loved the work so much she went back for two more summers.

Forbes's writing improved through her studies at Wisconsin. She also was on the editorial board of the *Wisconsin Literary*

Magazine, where she became good friends with fellow writer Marjorie Kinnan. Kinnan later became Marjorie Kinnan Rawlings and moved to Florida, where she wrote the much-acclaimed book, *The Yearling*.

Back to Boston

Forbes later said that going to Wisconsin was "one of the best moves I ever made. It gave me a chance to see my background with detachment and perspective."[14] But in 1919, it was time to return home. Through a friend, she learned of a position open at Houghton Mifflin Company, a Boston publisher. Forbes applied and was hired to be the assistant to the editor-in-chief of the trade department. Because her spelling was so bad, she was unsuited for secretarial work, so she became a reader of unsolicited manuscripts. At this she excelled. For example, she received a long novel that had been rejected by eleven publishers. It was a historical adventure set during the French Revolution, and Forbes believed that, if cut and edited, it could be an exciting story. She was right. The book was *Scaramouche* by Rafael Sabatini, and it not only sold well, but went on to become a popular movie.

Forbes also continued her own writing in the form of feature articles for the *Boston Evening Transcript*. She wrote about New England literary

Janet Leigh and Stewart Granger starred in the 1952 movie Scaramouche.

history and did profiles of authors. From her reading of manu-scripts submitted to Houghton Mifflin, she was also learning what *not* to do in writing a novel. Using those insights, she began to write a novel of her own.

During this busy time, she shared a Cambridge apartment with two other young women. They decided that to expand their social lives, they would host a dinner party each week to which each of them would invite a young man. It was at one of these dinners that Forbes met Albert Hoskins, a Harvard Law School student, whom she would marry in January 1926. "That was a busy time," she told a *New York Times Book Review* interviewer. "I was writing my first published novel, doing a full-time job, and getting engaged to be married. I almost never got to bed before three in the morning but it didn't hurt me in the least—never felt better."[15]

Early Published Novels

A few months after her marriage, Forbes's first published novel, *O Genteel Lady!* appeared. Set in the mid-1800s, it is about a young lady torn between "prevailing standards of Victorian behavior and her own natural impulses and sexual passions."[16] Forbes said she was inspired by reading old copies of *Godey's Lady's Book,* a popular woman's magazine in the 1800s, that she had found in her parents' attic. She was fascinated by the extravagantly dressed ladies with their hair in ringlets and by the interesting "contrast between mor-bid delicacy and pompous vulgarity"[17] in the magazine's stories.

The novel received favorable reviews, many already noting Forbes's ability to bring a distant time period to life. A *Boston Herald* reviewer wrote, "The author so faithfully recreates the life and thought of an earlier generation," and the *New York Times Book Review* said, "Miss Forbes has caught and kept throughout the charm of the bygone days she describes. She has captured the elu-sive lace and lavender element without its mustiness."[18] *O Genteel Lady!* was chosen by the newly formed Book-of-the-Month Club as its third selection in June. Within a month, it had sold twenty-five thousand copies and went on to become a best-seller.

A witch is condemned in seventeenth-century Salem. Fascinated with witches since childhood, Forbes wrote A Mirror for Witches, *published in 1928.*

By that time, Forbes had returned from a long wedding trip to Europe and had moved to New York, where her new husband began work at a law firm. Forbes had already started working on a new novel, *A Mirror for Witches,* which was also inspired by material in her parents' attic—volumes of information on witches and demonology. She said that even as a child, she "was mad about witches. My mother stitched little red devils on my handkerchiefs."[19] She also reminded readers about her ancestor, Rebecca Chamberlain, who died in jail while she waited to be tried as a witch in Cambridge in the late 1600s.

A Mirror for Witches was published in 1928, again to excellent reviews. Totally different from *O Genteel Lady!,* this novel is a dark tale of a young girl accused of witchcraft in seventeenth-century Salem. The main character is Doll Bilby, a young English girl who witnesses her parents' burning at the stake as witches. Sea captain Jared Bilby adopts her and takes her to Salem, Massachusetts, with his wife, Hannah. Hannah turns against the young girl, however, and tells the townspeople that Doll is a witch. Eventually, Doll comes to believe the lie herself and further believes that she is possessed by a demon lover. She dies giving birth in prison.

Doll's story is told by a narrator looking back a generation later, someone who really didn't know or understand all that had happened. Forbes wanted modern readers to see for themselves his misinterpretations. She also wanted them to see that Doll eventually found comfort and even fulfillment in the imaginary world she created for herself. "Certainly one of the basic ideas in the book," she said, "is that we all live, and endure, strengthened not so much perhaps by reality as by what we believe to be the truth."[20] Many critics have called *A Mirror for Witches* Forbes's best work of fiction, and it has been made into a ballet, a musical play, an opera, and a movie.

Forbes's interest in witches and witchcraft continued throughout her life. When she died, she was halfway through a definitive history of witchcraft in the seventeenth century.

Divorce and a Return to Home

The same year that *A Mirror for Witches* was published, Forbes and her husband moved back to the Boston area when Hoskins took a job as a probation officer. By then, however, the marriage was in trouble. Biographer Margaret Erskine writes, "Albert was, to put it bluntly, jealous of her writing. He would never allow her to write when he was in the house. She would send him off to work in the morning, write at a furious pace until noon, and then tend to her household duties in the latter part of the day."[21] Finally, in 1933, the couple divorced. Forbes decided to return to the family home in Worcester, where her mother still lived with Forbes's brother Allen and sister Cornelia (her father had died two years earlier). In addition, her sister Katharine lived just two doors away with her husband and four children. Forbes knew that a writer's life could be lonely, and she preferred to find company in the warmth of her family rather than in literary circles.

According to Erskine, the arrangement proved ideal. Forbes had a bedroom on the second floor and a writing room just above.

She preferred working in the mornings, and would fix a thermos of coffee at night to drink as soon as she got up in the morning. High on the third floor, she was away from household activity and could work steadily, without distractions, until late morning.

Forbes would write a first draft in longhand, using a form of shorthand she had developed for herself. She wrote as quickly as possible, believing that it gave her writing a "certain freshness."[22] She would then type what she had written. It was important that she not wait too long between the writing and the typing, because if she did, sometimes she couldn't read her own writing. Later in her life, she found an assistant to do this typing for her, but for years she did it herself. Erskine describes how research sometimes became a family affair:

> She would have quantities of notes spread all over her writing room and sometimes expanding into the bedroom. At times maps of Boston or Salem would be spread

Forbes would pore over old maps like this one when doing research for a book.

out in the dining room and the whole family would work on deciding where old roads once ran. She traveled about to do research and get the feel of places, sometimes alone, sometimes with her mother, or, later on, with a nephew or niece. She worked every morning, almost without fail.

By late morning she was ready to come downstairs and join in the busy social life of the family.[23]

Forbes herself talked about her writing habits in a *New York Times Book Review* interview:

Of course, I enjoy writing, always have. I like the pile of paper, the sharpened pencils, and use them rapidly—writing in my own shorthand. I let myself go in the first draft because you can cut and chop as much as you like later, but if the first draft doesn't have vitality, you might as well abandon the whole project. It is wasteful to write about four times as much as I ever can use, but that seems to be the only way in which I can find out what it is that I need. Then I cut and re-do and fool with it until the publisher takes it away from me.[24]

Paradise, Miss Marvel, and *The General's Lady*

Once settled at home, Forbes concentrated on her next novel, a long saga named *Paradise* that followed the lives of a family in colonial Massachusetts. When the manuscript ran over one thousand pages, Forbes realized that she had lost her focus. She put *Paradise* aside to write another, shorter novel, *Miss Marvel*. Written in just ten days, it was about two eccentric sisters in New England. It received favorable reviews, but Forbes never liked it, referring to it as "chintzy."[25]

Still, the time away from *Paradise* was good for Forbes. Coming back to the novel, she was able to see clearly what she wanted to do, and she finished the book in six months. "I never spent a happier six months,"[26] she said. But she was soon faced with another dilemma. Houghton Mifflin, her publisher, thought the manuscript was too long and wanted Forbes to cut it, as well as make major revisions to the story. According to Erskine, this presented a real crisis for Forbes. She believed in her book and would rather see it go unpublished than be forced to make revisions that would change the meaning of her work. In the end, she withdrew *Paradise* from Houghton Mifflin and offered it to Harcourt Brace, which published it in 1937. "It was a tremendous success," said her sister Katharine in a 1979 interview, "and Houghton Mifflin felt terrible."[27]

Forbes's next novel, *The General's Lady*, was published in 1938. It was based on the true story of Bathsheba Spooner, who had been hanged in Worcester, along with three men, for the murder of her husband, a general with the colonial army during the American Revolution. Forbes fictionalized the story and created the character of Morganna Bale, a young woman in a Tory family who marries an American general in order to save her family's fortune. She then has an affair with a British officer and plots to kill her husband.

Once again many reviews commented on Forbes's historic accuracy and ability to bring the past to life. Some of those reviews were written by successful fellow writers. Stephen Vincent Benet, who received a Pulitzer Prize for his epic poem *John Brown's Body*, wrote in the *Saturday Review of Literature*, "The historical background, as is usual with Miss Forbes, is done with great skill and ease. The people are always people . . . in the genuine costume of the time. Nor does Miss Forbes make the mistake of transferring twentieth-century customs and prejudices to the eighteenth." And Walter Edmonds, author of the Revolutionary War novel *Drums Along the Mohawk*, wrote in a letter to Harcourt Brace, "I know of no one except Esther Forbes herself who can make the Colonial [period] so intimate and tie the authentic life of that day so closely to her story."[28]

Forbes at Home

Forbes worked hard during the mornings, but afternoons were devoted to other pursuits. She loved gardening and turned what had once been a tennis court into a lovely perennial garden. More important were family and friends. "Writing's a solitary sort of thing," she said, "and when writers get out, they naturally want to see as many people as they can."[29] She was known as a gracious hostess around Worcester and became well-known for her parties. After *The General's Lady* was published, she gave a party to which she invited descendants of those involved in Bathsheba Spooner's trial. One direct descendant of the presiding judge retold the story to Forbes's guests.

Esther Forbes, seen here in 1937, typically wrote in the morning and spent afternoons and evenings pursuing hobbies and socializing.

Over the years, Forbes used income from her books to make improvements to the family home in Worcester. According to Erskine, she remodeled the kitchen with funds from the sale of English rights to *Paradise*, and from then on called the kitchen "the English kitchen." The refurbished guest room became known as "Paul Revere's room" and a sofa in the living room was called "Paul's sofa."

World War II and Paul Revere

When *The General's Lady* was published, Forbes was already working on another book about the American Revolution. She planned to write about a person who remained neutral during the war, someone who could see both sides. Then came World War II and everything changed. She explained:

> I thought that I had a fine character. Then the Nazis attacked Poland and I was suddenly the most unneutral woman in the world. That destroyed all that I'd been writing about. A person who could stay neutral in war! The character was absurd. But I had a great deal of research completed—that is, my mother had done an enormous amount of research for me, and I'd done a lot—so I wrote of Revere and his world.[30]

The initial idea of the biography was presented to Forbes by Houghton Mifflin. Once committed, Forbes enlisted further help from her mother, who was now in her mid-eighties. The two women spent hours at the Massachusetts Historical Society as well as at the American Antiquarian Society in Worcester. In fact, they spent so much time in a corner off the reading room at the Antiquarian Society that it became known as the "Forbes Alcove." So closely did mother and daughter work that when *Paul Revere and the World He Lived In* won the Pulitzer Prize in history in 1943, Forbes insisted that her mother receive much of the credit.

Patriot and silversmith Paul Revere was the subject of Forbes's Pulitzer Prize–winning novel, Paul Revere and the World He Lived In.

Forbes approached Paul Revere differently from other biographers. Others had written about the intellectual Revere; she perceived him as an ordinary man—a family man and an artisan—who had lived a simple life until the events of the Revolution thrust him into a different role. She said, "Paul Revere, who went to work when he was 13 years old, represented the average man. Without him, of course the Revolution would have gone on anyway. But there were hundreds of men in this country just like Revere—and without them there wouldn't have been a Revolution."[31]

The book received excellent reviews. As always, Forbes's ability to bring the past to life was especially noted. In a front-page review, the *New York Times Book Review* said that *Paul Revere and the World He Lived In* was

> one of the best books of this or any generation about the period of the American Revolution. . . . Esther Forbes writes not so much like a historian who has done creditable research as [like] a woman, home-loving but of wide interests, who actually lived in Boston between—say— 1757 and 1818. She writes like a person who has kept house in a Boston home of the period, not like a costumed guide who shows people around.[32]

Johnny Tremain **Is Born**

In addition to bringing her the Pulitzer Prize, the Paul Revere biography was the inspiration for her sole novel for young people, *Johnny Tremain*. During her research she became interested in the lives of Boston apprentices and their role in the Revolution. Forbes also felt the novelist's frustration at having to stick to the facts, when her imagination longed to fill in the blanks of unanswered questions. She told a *New York Times Book Review* interviewer:

> The biographer . . . assembles his clues, follows this scent and then another, working always from the outside in—while the novelist starts at the very center. And yet no matter how hard the biographer works, those innermost secrets, with which the novelist starts, are forever unsolved. I've not the faintest idea, for instance, why Paul Revere married Sara Orne. I don't know why he was so fond of horses. . . . And what was he doing at a wedding party so soon after [Sara's] death having a good time, too? There is so much that doesn't fit.[33]

As a biographer she couldn't answer those questions, but she promised herself that when she was finished with the biography, she would write a novel. That novel was *Johnny Tremain*.

When the *Johnny Tremain* manuscript was finished, Forbes sent it to Harcourt Brace, which had published her last novel, *Paradise*. But this time, the Harcourt editor made extensive changes, not only cutting the book in length, but shortening sentences to fit the convention for children's books and even changing the scenes in which Johnny grows and changes. Forbes was deeply disappointed and wrote to her agent:

Forbes was disappointed in the changes Harcourt Brace wanted to make to Johnny Tremain.

What I do definitely want is to have you get me out of the contract—as politely and tactfully as only you can. . . . There are a number of things . . . that could be cut but what I object to is cutting almost all of the paragraphs and scenes which show his changing relationship to many of the people with whom he is thrown. For if I had one predominating thought in mind while writing the book it was to show this flux and change. . . . I hoped by so doing to give a young reader a feeling of actuality—that these were real people such as he himself knew.[34]

Forbes was also upset by the suggested word changes. She always tried to give her readers a feel for real speech, and objected to changing expressions such as "barged in" to "walked in," "snitching" to "stealing," and "rattled" to "nervous." In the end, Harcourt returned the manuscript to Forbes, who sent it to Houghton Mifflin. It was published with few changes in 1943 and became an instant success, winning the prestigious Newbery Award in 1944. It is still considered a classic of young people's literature.

Return to Editing and More Writing

With so many men in the armed forces during World War II, Houghton Mifflin was shorthanded and asked Forbes to return as an editor. This she did, commuting two or three days a week to Boston from 1942 to 1946. She also worked on two nonfiction books. One was a children's biography, *America's Paul Revere*, published in 1946; it was illustrated by Lynd Ward, who did illustrations for *Johnny Tremain*. The other was *The Boston Book*, a pictorial essay put together with photographer Arthur Griffin, which was published in 1947.

Forbes's heart, however, was in fiction, and she was also working on a long historical novel about Salem, Massachusetts, set in the late 1700s and early 1800s. Published in 1948 as *The Running of the Tide*, the book tells the story of the Inman family, a wealthy

Clark Gable was set to star in the movie version of The Running of the Tide, *but the film was never made.*

family of ship owners. The theme of the book, she said, was "the glory of youth [represented in part by a ship's figurehead] . . . slowly giving way to time. One of the sad but inevitable facts of life. Notice the book begins with the figurehead's first taste of salt water. The last sentence is also hers."[35]

As usual for Forbes's novels, reviews were good. *The Running of the Tide* also won the Metro-Goldwyn-Mayer (MGM) prize for the best novel of the year, which the film studio then planned to make into a movie. The movie was to star Clark Gable, who had played the romantic Rhett Butler in *Gone with the Wind* in 1939, but the movie was never made. Nor was the prize ever given again because of financial problems in the movie industry. Still, Forbes received $150,000 in prize money and celebrated in an uncharacteristically extravagant way by buying herself a mink stole.

Family Responsibilities and Last Novel

In the late 1940s, Forbes's mother, who was in her nineties, became an invalid, leaving Forbes and her sister Cornelia responsible for the household and for supervising their mother's care. Forbes had little time to write until her mother's death in 1951. But then she began what would be her last novel, *Rainbow on the Road*, published in 1954. The book followed one season in the life of a "limner," a folk artist in the 1830s. Limners would paint portrait backgrounds and then spend their springs and summers traveling around the countryside, ready to paint portraits of people into their pictures. The novel had little plot, but reviewers praised its pastoral presentation of life in the New England countryside in the mid–nineteenth century.

Johnny Tremain Becomes a Movie

In the mid-1950s, Walt Disney decided to make a movie of *Johnny Tremain*. Forbes's biographer Margaret Erskine describes an interesting story behind the movie. Apparently, the Walt Disney studio had assembled a script, actors, and a set, and was ready to start production when someone realized no one had approached the author about purchasing the rights to the story. Erskine speculates that the oversight probably occurred because Disney films were usually based on stories, such as fairy tales, already in the public domain. Whatever the reason, the studio had to contact Forbes, who turned the negotiations over to Houghton Mifflin. In the end, she received only $5,000 for the movie rights. She did, however, refuse permission for any adaptation or shortened version of the book to be published.

Although the movie followed the plot line, it lacked the depth of the book. Action was emphasized, issues simplified, and Johnny's

The Disney movie Johnny Tremain *differed from Forbes's book in that it emphasized action over character development.*

growth as a person, the key element in the novel, was lost. Disney also changed Forbes's ending, leaving Rab alive and continuing the story beyond the novel, with Rab and Johnny participating in the Battle of Concord. Erskine says that Forbes was "not completely happy with the movie, but never pretended to know anything about the making of one."[36]

Last Years

After the publication of *Rainbow on the Road*, Forbes returned to a favorite project—the history of witchcraft in seventeenth-century Massachusetts. In 1960, she became the first woman elected to the American Antiquarian Society in Worcester, an organization that collects and preserves records for public use. As the 1960s progressed, Forbes's health began to fail. She had always had heart problems from her bout with rheumatic fever as a child, but her irregular heartbeat began to bother her more and more. She was only half finished with her history of witchcraft when she died of rheumatic heart disease on August 12, 1967. She was seventy-six years old.

Forbes left the royalties of her works to the American Antiquarian Society in thanks for all the help she had received in her research. The society still receives her fan mail, often letters from students who have read *Johnny Tremain* in school. Each letter is answered and the writer receives a copy of the organization's long obituary of Forbes.

Today, Forbes is remembered more for *Johnny Tremain* than for her other books. But during her time, Forbes's books were widely read and praised for their attention to historic detail and for the life she put into her characters. They were translated into ten languages and many were reprinted as paperbacks. The *New York Times* summarized her talent when it said in its obituary that Forbes, "a novelist who wrote like a historian and a historian who wrote like a novelist, achieved a reputation as one of the most exciting and knowledgeable authors on the Revolutionary era."[37]

A Novel for Turbulent Times

E sther Forbes's only novel for young people is set in the turbulent times of pre-Revolutionary Boston. It begins in the
summer of 1773, six months before the Boston Tea Party.
At that time, Boston was a city deeply divided between the Whigs,
or Patriots—who wanted the colonies to be more self-governing—
and the Tories, or Loyalists—who believed that the colonies should
accept the authority of the British Parliament and king. Taxes were
a major issue. The Whigs did not wish to pay taxes that the British
imposed without the colonies' consent. "No taxation without rep-
resentation" became their rallying cry. Trouble had been brewing
for almost ten years, as colonists had protested taxes levied in 1765
and 1767.

To counter the antitax protests, the British government quartered almost two thousand troops in Boston, causing even more
tension. Some Patriots banded together to form a secret society
called the Sons of Liberty, that sometimes resorted to mob action
to intimidate Tories. In 1770, British soldiers fired on an angry
mob, killing five men and wounding six. The soldiers were tried for
murder, but Patriot lawyer John Adams agreed to represent them,
believing strongly in the rule of law. He won an acquittal by
demonstrating to the jury that the men had acted in self-defense.

Still, the event became known as the Boston Massacre, and many Boston citizens bitterly resented the military occupation of their city.

However, for the next few years relations between the colonies and the mother country calmed down, as both sides of the Atlantic experienced prosperity. Then, Britain passed the Tea Act of 1773, which not only retained the American tax on tea, but gave the East India Tea Company the exclusive rights to sell tea in the colonies. Once again, a power struggle developed between the colonists and Britain. The Sons of Liberty and other Patriot leaders insisted the East India tea would not be sold in the colonies. In Boston, Patriots took matters into their own hands, dumping tea into the harbor at the now well-known Boston Tea Party.

Leading the Patriots in Boston were men such as Sam Adams, an unsuccessful businessman but successful politician; John Adams, the lawyer and second cousin to Sam Adams; John Hancock, a wealthy merchant; Dr. Joseph Warren, a respected physician; James Otis, a lawyer and politician; and Paul Revere, a silversmith and prominent member of Boston's Sons of Liberty. All of these famous men appear in *Johnny Tremain*, brought to vivid life by Forbes's extensive knowledge of them and their times.

Parallels with World War II

The times in which Esther Forbes wrote *Johnny Tremain* could also be called turbulent. It was 1943 and the entire country was mobilized in fighting World War II. Although the United States was not occupied by a foreign power, Germany, Japan, and their Axis partners were trampling upon the rights and freedoms of other nations. And when finally attacked by Japan, Americans were quick to join the beleaguered countries fighting to maintain their liberty. Patriotic feelings were strong as young men—and sometimes young women—risked their lives for the ideals of freedom. For Forbes, these ideals echoed those of the Patriots in Revolutionary times. She saw parallels between the two wars as she wrote her novel about a young silversmith.

In her acceptance paper and speech for the Newbery Medal, Forbes said the young fighting men of World War II had much in common with the nineteen-year-olds who served during the Revolutionary War. Although they might have been considered "boys" in peacetime, wartime forced them to become men. They faced not only adult responsibilities but the possibility of adult loss, for some would lose family members or friends in the fighting. For that reason, Forbes explained, she had Johnny lose his best friend at Lexington.

Forbes also wanted to show the World War II generation how another generation faced war and hardship. "I . . . wanted to show that these earlier boys were conscious of what they were fighting for and that it was something which they believed was worth more than their own lives," she added. "And to show that many of the issues at stake in this war are the same as in the earlier one. We are still fighting for simple things 'that a man may stand up.'"[38]

Esther Forbes felt the young men serving in World War II had a lot in common with the young men who fought in the Revolutionary War.

Lives of Apprentices

But while the theme of fighting for the "rights of man" is important in *Johnny Tremain*, it evolves from the story; it is not the reason Forbes wrote the book. *Johnny Tremain* grew from Forbes's interest in the lives of apprentices in colonial Boston's shops and wharves. She researched their lives when writing her Paul Revere biography, beginning with the life of Revere's father, Apollos Rivoire, later Americanized to Paul Revere "merely on account that the bumpkins pronounce it easier,"[39] he said. Apollos Rivoire's parents had sent him away from France at the age of thirteen to escape religious persecution. He was apprenticed to a famous Boston goldsmith, and later struck out on his own. Forbes wondered what young Rivoire was like, just as she wondered about his famous son, Paul Revere. She longed to make up characters to answer her own questions, but she couldn't do that in a biography. And so the idea for the character of Johnny Tremain was born. "I promised myself that sometime I would write a story and make up anything I wanted as long as I kept it typical of the period," she said. "Then I would know not merely what was done but why and how people felt."[40]

In her research, for example, she learned that apprentices played a large role in the Boston Tea Party. The Patriot leaders were afraid the tea company might sue if they recognized perpetrators, so they wanted the work to be done by those without property. Who better to use than poor apprentices? "And how they must have enjoyed themselves!"[41] Forbes speculated. In a biography, she couldn't put feelings into the heads of these young men, but in a novel she could. *Johnny Tremain* presents a vivid account of that historic night, including Johnny's anticipation and involvement in the excitement.

Roots of the Title Character

Forbes's title character, Johnny Tremain, sprang from historical fact as well. She learned that it was a horse boy who brought the news to Paul Revere that the British were marching on the night

By making the characters of Johnny (left) and Rab young apprentices, Forbes was able to place them in the middle of the action during the Boston Tea Party.

of April 18. The young boy worked at a stable near British general and colonial governor Thomas Gage's headquarters. Like Johnny, he made friends with the horse boys of the British officers. When one of them unintentionally revealed that the British were marching that night, the young Patriot ran to Revere with the information. Forbes said that she wondered about those two boys, one British, one Patriot. "Did they really like each other or not? Were they bright boys or stupid boys?"[42] She didn't know and she couldn't speculate in her biography, but a novel would be different. There, she could provide answers.

In her writing, Forbes also wanted to share her excitement about human nature, how people are always changing and never predictable. She didn't believe in the prevailing attitude toward children's books—that heroes had to be all good, and villains all evil. She wanted her readers to see real people in her characters. In talking about Johnny, Forbes said:

> In planning the story I wanted to give Johnny room enough to change and grow; not clamp down upon him

certain characteristics as unchanging as Little Orphan Annie's optimism. I did not want him to be more consistent than people are in life. If he was courageous, he also felt fear. Affectionate, but he could also hate. Talkative, but sometimes he said the wrong things, or too much, or even too little. Nor were his feelings for the people about him to be unchanging. . . . When Johnny realizes Dove is responsible for his burned hand he swears (and he means it) that he is going to get him for that. . . . But in less than two years . . . in the casual way of normal human beings he has really forgotten his oath of vengeance. He even— rather patronizingly—befriends Dove, who has not a friend in the world. Nor are Johnny's relations with the older and much-admired Rab quite as perfect as boys' friendships are apt to be in books. To the very end Rab baffles him, holds him at arm's length. So in other ways I have tried to show human nature is less rigid, more fascinating, than in, say comic strips.[43]

Pushing Johnny to grow and change is his burned hand, which he suffered by the spiteful act of another apprentice jealous of Johnny's talents. Forbes said that she wanted to give Johnny an obstacle that would have a psychological effect—the destruction of all of his dreams and plans—not just a physical effect. She chose the burned hand because it was simple enough for a small child to understand, yet had devastating consequences that would give Johnny a chance to show his courage. Unlike modern times, where social agencies would provide help to a young person with Johnny's problems, eighteenth-century young people were forced to rely on their own determination and resources.

More Complex Relationships

Not only did Forbes want Johnny to appear real and human, but she also wanted the British soldiers to be seen as people who tried to be decent in a difficult situation. She believed that American schools too often portrayed the British soldiers as total villains, while in fact, history shows that their occupation of Boston from 1774 to 1776 was marked by a fairness not usually shown to an occupied city. There were no arrests of rebel leaders, no hangings, no concentration camps, and no shooting of local citizens. In British eyes, leaders like John Hancock, Sam Adams, and Dr. Joseph Warren were certainly committing high treason, yet they were allowed to remain free and continue their rebellious activities.

Forbes hoped that her young readers would contrast the British behavior with the horrors of Nazi-occupied Europe. "The contrast . . . [with] what the Nazis are doing today is startling," she said. "And I really wanted young people today to think of the British in Boston—and the Nazis in, say, Rotterdam [in occupied Holland]."[44] Like all good historical novelists, she was using the past to help her readers better understand the present.

Having written Johnny Tremain *during World War II, Forbes hoped that her readers would contrast the British occupation of Boston with the Nazi occupation of Europe.*

Johnny Tremain **Captures Its Audience**

Johnny Tremain was an immediate critical success. It received excellent reviews, as well as the Newbery Medal for excellence in children's literature in 1944. Many prestigious magazines and newspapers praised its historical realism and believable characters. The *Horn Book* called the work "an outstanding novel of Revolutionary days in Boston," citing its "details of domestic life, its penetrating knowledge of colonial Boston, its perception of character, its artistry."[45]

All the research that Forbes had done for her Paul Revere biography was poured into her descriptions in *Johnny Tremain*. The *New Yorker* magazine called it "a distinguished and continually interesting story. . . . There is a living sense of America's past in the

Johnny Tremain *received such praise that one critic noted that the character of Johnny could be held in the same high regard as Mark Twain's Huck Finn (pictured).*

book."[46] The *Saturday Review of Literature* said, "Esther Forbes's power to create, and to recreate, a face, a voice, a scene takes us as living spectators to the Boston Tea Party, to the Battles of Lexington and of North Creek. . . . Over and over again, we share some little incident that makes those days in Boston as exciting and as vital as Washington and London and Moscow are today."[47]

Nor did the critics ignore Forbes's characterization, praising the "aliveness" of her characters, especially Johnny. *Book Week* said, "This is Esther Forbes at her brilliant best. She has drawn the character of Johnny with such sympathy and insight that he may well take his place with Jim Hawkins, Huck Finn and other young immortals."[48] And the *New York Times Book Review* devoted almost an entire page to the book:

> Miss Forbes not only knows the wharves, the inns, the very cobblestones of eighteenth-century Boston about as intimately as her own back yard, but . . . she creates three-dimensional people. Historical figures are clothed in flesh as well as good broadcloth, even casual street figures are endowed for the moment of their appearance with reality, and thus we see the temper of a city and a period.

> Johnny Tremain, of course, we like all the better for his arrogance, his impudence, his boyish disregard of anybody's feelings but his own. After all, nobody except loyal Cilla, whom he rather casually expected to marry one day, cared very much about *his* feelings. . . . [*Johnny Tremain*] is a novel for the teen age, and as such the most distinguished one we have had in years.[49]

Many critics also saw the comparisons that Forbes was trying to make between the Revolutionary War and World War II. The *Horn Book*'s review noted the importance of the theme of liberty. It said about Johnny, "Quick-tongued Johnny is no prodigy, he plays no important role in memorable deeds, but he is a true, likable boy, growing up to manhood at sixteen, to understand, as many boys are understanding today, the meaning to all men of the Liberty for which they fight."[50]

The same critic, writing about Forbes after she won the Newbery Medal, said, "Out of the past comes the present. . . . Esther Forbes has brought to boys and girls a living spark from the fires that lighted the liberties that they are now called upon to defend."[51] Such idealism may be difficult for teenagers today to understand because they live in more skeptical times. But for teens who lived in a time totally involved in a war with widespread support, *Johnny Tremain* provided not only good historical fiction, but also inspiration. The novel told them where their ideals of freedom came from and let them know that real people in an earlier time had also made sacrifices for freedom. Forbes emphasized her belief that some ideals were worth fighting for and even dying for. This sobering thought links the past and the present.

CHAPTER THREE

The Story of
Johnny
Tremain

Chapter 1: Up and About

Johnny Tremain begins with a typical morning in the Lapham household in Boston. The year is 1773. Mr. Lapham is a silversmith whose skill has been declining with age. His son is dead and his widowed daughter-in-law, Mrs. Lapham, keeps the house running. To do so, she depends on her father-in-law's talented apprentice, fourteen-year-old Johnny Tremain, to see that the silver work gets done. It is Johnny's skill and hard work that support Mr. and Mrs. Lapham as well as Mrs. Lapham's four daughters: Madge, eighteen; Dorcas, sixteen; Priscilla (Cilla), fourteen; and Isannah, eight. Johnny is so tied into the family's well-being that it is assumed that someday he and Cilla will marry.

Johnny is well aware of his talent and his important place in the Lapham household, and he bullies his fellow apprentices, Dove and Dusty. Dusty is younger than Johnny; he is eager but lacks the older boy's talent. Dove is an older but clumsy boy. He is especially resentful of Johnny's bullying. Even Mr. Lapham, a pious man, sees Johnny's arrogant behavior and often warns him about the sin of pride. Still, when wealthy John Hancock orders a silver sugar bowl to replace a broken one and Mr. Lapham hesitates, no one objects when Johnny takes charge and says they can do it.

While Johnny devotes himself to Mr. Hancock's bowl and other projects, other aspects of Johnny's life are revealed. One hot night, when Isannah can't sleep, Johnny takes her and Cilla to the end of the wharf to feel the cool sea air. There he tells Cilla that his full name is Jonathan *Lyte* Tremain. His mother had told him he was related to the wealthy merchant Jonathan Lyte, and that if he were ever so low that he had nowhere to turn, he was to seek help from Mr. Lyte. To prove that he is telling the truth, he shows Cilla a silver cup his mother had given to him. On the cup is the rising eye symbol of the Lytes and the motto, "Let there be Lyte."

Chapter 2: The Pride of Your Power

As the week progresses, Johnny struggles to complete the sugar bowl for John Hancock. By Saturday afternoon the handles are

Johnny shows Cilla the silver cup he received from his mother.

ready to cast. But Dove delays bringing the charcoal for the fire, and Johnny yells at him for wasting precious time. Mr. Lapham scolds Johnny for his pride and declares that work will stop for the day. Johnny, mindful of the deadline, is frantic. It is illegal to work the next day, Sunday, because it is the Sabbath, a day of worship. With the deadline seven o'clock Monday morning, the sugar bowl would never be finished in time. But pious Mr. Lapham doesn't care if the order is delivered or not.

Mrs. Lapham, however, does care, and when Mr. Lapham leaves for a deacons' meeting Sunday afternoon, she puts the apprentices back to work. All goes well until Dove, angry with Johnny, hands Johnny a cracked crucible into which to pour the silver. When the crucible breaks and molten silver starts running down over the furnace, Johnny reaches out with his right hand and loses his footing. His right hand lands in the melted silver on the furnace and is severely burned.

Because they were breaking the Sabbath, Mrs. Lapham calls Gran' Hopper, an old midwife, instead of a doctor to treat the burn. The old woman soothes the burn and gives Johnny medicine for the pain, but when she wraps the hand, she allows the thumb to bend in toward the palm. This is less painful for Johnny, but weeks later, when the hand is healed and the bandage is removed, scar tissue has bound his thumb to his palm. Johnny's hand is crippled. His career as a silversmith is over.

For a while everyone is sympathetic. Johnny wanders around idly. Then Mrs. Lapham begins calling him names like "lazy good-for-nothing" and "lug-a-bed."[52] Soon he must start earning his keep. No longer the talented favorite, he does menial chores like fetching water and charcoal. Dove and Dusty laugh at him. Mr. Lapham tells Johnny that he will never turn him out, but that Johnny must look for another trade. Johnny also learns that Dove deliberately gave him the cracked crucible. Mr. Lapham says Dove meant only to humiliate him, not injure him, but Johnny still swears revenge.

Chapter 3: An Earth of Brass

Johnny tries unsuccessfully to find a new trade. One day in September he passes by the newspaper office of the *Boston Observer*. He likes the sign, so he walks in and meets apprentice Rab Silsbee. He is won over by Rab's easygoing manner and tells him his story. Rab says the *Observer* is looking for a delivery boy, and that Johnny can come back if he finds nothing else. Johnny continues his search.

In the meantime, Johnny's inability to work has created a huge need in the Lapham household. Old Mr. Lapham is now more interested in preparing for the "next world" than in taking care of his business in this one. To ensure that the silversmith shop survives, Mrs. Lapham negotiates with silversmith Percival Tweedie to come into the business. Mr. Tweedie is single, and Mrs. Lapham expects him to marry one of the Lapham daughters and keep the business in the family.

When Tweedie arrives at the Laphams', Johnny insults him, causing Mrs. Lapham to throw Johnny out. Johnny wanders around the wharves and sees Lavinia Lyte, daughter of merchant Jonathan Lyte, getting off a ship from England, where she has spent the summer. He is taken with her beauty, but he is also resentful of her wealth. Johnny tries to apprentice himself to John Hancock as a clerk, but then cannot write because of his crippled hand and is sent away. Hancock, however, sends his servant after Johnny to give him a bag of silver.

Johnny is hungry and spends most of the money on a huge lunch. He is immediately sorry. But he has enough left to buy a new pair of shoes for himself and gifts for Cilla and Isannah. When he goes home, Mrs. Lapham accuses him of stealing. Isannah recoils from the touch of his crippled hand and screams at him to go away. Cilla slaps her, but still, Johnny leaves. This is his low point. He believes that Isannah said what everyone else was thinking. Johnny goes to his mother's grave and sobs. He sleeps and then awakens suddenly. His mother's words come to him. If he ever had nothing left and even God had turned away,

Johnny meets Rab for the first time in the office of the Boston Observer.

he was to go to Mr. Lyte. A feeling of peace comes over him. When day comes, he will take his silver cup to merchant Lyte at his office on Long Wharf.

Chapter 4: The Rising Eye

Mr. Lyte doesn't believe Johnny when the boy says he is a relative. Johnny states that he has a silver cup from the family to prove he is telling the truth. Mr. Lyte invites him to bring the cup to his home in the evening. Johnny is sure he'll be rich by nightfall. On his way to the Lytes', he stops in to see Rab. Rab warns him that Lyte is crooked and says that he tries to be on both sides, Tory and Whig, of the political turmoil in the colonies. Johnny knows nothing of politics, but he learns that Rab is a Whig, or Patriot, and is opposed to many of the king's policies in America. Rab lends him a shirt and jacket to wear to the Lytes'.

Johnny is "welcomed" into the Lytes' living room, but when he produces the cup, he is arrested for theft by an awaiting sheriff. Mr. Lyte lies, saying the cup was stolen in August. He also points out that Johnny's apprentice contract with the Laphams shows no Lyte in Johnny's name. Johnny is taken to jail. He knows he could be hanged for stealing. Rab arrives in the morning to help. Johnny sees a Sons of Liberty medal around Rab's neck. The jailer is also in the Sons of Liberty and Johnny is treated well. He tells Rab the whole story, and Rab says that Josiah Quincy, a respected young lawyer, will help him.

Meanwhile Mr. Lyte tries to bribe the Laphams into keeping Cilla from testifying for Johnny, but Rab tricks Mrs. Lapham into letting Cilla come with him. In court, she testifies that she had seen Johnny's cup in July, a month before its alleged theft. Coached by Rab, Isannah also comes to court and swears she saw the cup, too. Johnny is released and given back his cup. Isannah kisses Johnny's injured hand.

Chapter 5: The *Boston Observer*

Johnny is free, but has no place to live. He decides to sell his cup to Mr. Lyte. But Mr. Lyte takes the cup from Johnny and has an associate try to kidnap him to sea. Johnny escapes the trap and runs to Rab and the *Boston Observer*. Rab makes good on his promise and gets Johnny hired to deliver the papers on horseback. Johnny learns to ride Goblin, a skittish horse that comes to trust him. Johnny starts to love his three days of delivering papers each week, especially when he goes out to the villages in the country-side.

Now living in the loft above the print shop with Rab, Johnny is also welcomed into Rab's family. Uncle Lorne and Aunt Jenifer are kind to him, and on days when he isn't riding, they open up their home and library to him. Johnny becomes fond of Goblin and takes over caring for the horse at the stable of the Afric Queen tavern. The owners of the Afric Queen also hire Johnny to deliver messages.

Johnny is happy, but still a little homesick for life with the Laphams. One day he sees Cilla at the city pump fetching water in two big buckets. He helps her carry the water and agrees to meet her every Thursday and Sunday.

Johnny and Rab become friends, but Rab always keeps part of himself hidden. Still, he is a good influence, once casually asking Johnny, "Why do you go out of your way to make bad feeling? . . . Was it fun . . . going about letting everybody who got in your way have it?"[53] Johnny learns to control his anger. For example,

he holds his tongue when Patriot leader Sam Adams's servant accidentally douses him with water. His reward is a piece of apple pie and a chance to meet Sam Adams himself. Adams later asks Johnny to deliver messages for the Boston Committee of Correspondence. (The Boston Committee of Correspondence was one of many such political committees in the colonies. Patriot leaders in different colonies would write to each other, so that leaders in one colony would know about events and problems in the others.)

Chapter 6: Salt-Water Tea

Sam Adams awakens Johnny and Rab one Sunday morning in late November 1773 and asks Rab to print a flyer.

Johnny delivered messages for Patriot leader and politician, Sam Adams.

The first of the British tea ships is arriving, and the Patriots are calling a meeting to plan a response. Many colonists believe that the tax on tea—the last remaining tax levied by Parliament—is unfair and they refuse to pay it. To prevent collection of the tax, the Patriots are determined that the tea will not be unloaded. Johnny is sent off to summon the Observers—a secret Patriot organization—to a meeting that night in the loft of the print shop. That afternoon, he meets Cilla and Isannah at the water pump. Now, however, Cilla's humdrum news bores him for he feels that he is being caught up in larger, more important issues. Later, when he delivers the message to Patriot leader Dr. Joseph Warren, Warren offers to look at his hand. But Johnny does not show it to him.

That evening, Johnny recognizes a group of the Sons of Liberty beating a Tory. Although he supports the Whigs, Johnny feels sorry for the Tory whose only crime is his loyalty to Britain. Still, Johnny is swept up in the Patriot cause. At the Observers meeting, he and Rab learn about the plan to dump the tea into the harbor if the governor will not allow the tea to be returned to England. Rab is asked to organize a group of apprentices to do the actual work of boarding the ships and opening the crates of tea. Johnny is delighted that Rab includes him and starts to practice, using an ax in his left hand. He regrets not showing Warren his injured right hand.

December 16 is the last day for the governor to send the tea ships back to England. When he refuses, the Boston Tea Party begins. That night, a group of men and boys, many of them apprentices, dress up as Native Americans and board the tea ships. The "Indians" meet no resistance. Johnny sees Dove, who has sneaked in uninvited, trying to steal tea. He and Rab throw Dove into the harbor. The next day, all of Boston is talking about the tea. They are worried, too, because they know Britain will punish the city for this rebellious act.

Chapter 7: The Fiddler's Bill

Boston's punishment is more severe than expected. On June 1, 1774, the city's port—its lifeblood—is ordered closed until the

When Governor Hutchinson refused to return the tea shipment to England, the Observers organized the Boston Tea Party.

tea is paid for. Governor Hutchinson is recalled to England and British general Gage is put in charge of the colony. Additional British troops arrive to enforce the laws and quell further rebellion. Work and money become scarce as first the wharves, then the shops surrounding the wharf, and finally other businesses are idled. Even the *Observer* is affected, as the paper shrinks to half its previous size. Still, the city doesn't starve, as the other colonies, in support of Boston's defiance, send food and supplies by land.

General Gage does not arrest the known Patriots for treason; he still hopes problems between England and the colonies can be

With the arrival of more British troops, the Patriots organized themselves into militias just in case.

resolved peacefully. Many Patriots are not so optimistic. Citizen militias are organized in case England decides to use force. Rab joins the Lexington Minutemen and is obsessed with acquiring a good musket. Johnny agrees to carry messages for the British, in hopes that he can get information for the Patriots.

One day Johnny comes home to find Cilla at the *Observer*, laughing with Rab. He's annoyed that she's having so much fun with Rab. She tells him that Dorcas eloped with a suitor named Frizel, Junior, when Mr. Tweedie declared he wanted to marry her. Her biggest news, however, is that she and Isannah now live with the Lytes. Lavinia had been very taken with Isannah's beauty at a visit to the Laphams' and received permission from Mrs. Lapham for Isannah to go home with her. Since Isannah wouldn't go without Cilla, Cilla was included in the arrangement. Cilla, however, works in the house as a servant and is not doted on as Isannah is.

Some British officers take up residence in the Afric Queen tavern, and since Johnny still keeps Goblin there, he listens for gossip. He meets Lieutenant Stranger, who wants to commandeer Goblin for Colonel Smith. Not wanting to lose his horse, Johnny spooks the skittish Goblin so that he throws the lieutenant. The lieutenant takes the fall with good grace, and even offers to teach Johnny how to jump.

Johnny also meets Dove again, who is working as a stable boy for the British colonel Smith after being fired from the silversmith shop by Mr. Tweedie. But Johnny has changed and no longer wants revenge. He also rethinks his life at the Laphams and has a better understanding of how hard the widowed Mrs. Lapham worked to keep the household going for her daughters, her father-in-law, and the apprentices. He visits the Laphams to have Tweedie fix a spur for him. He sees Madge in the garden, clearly in love with Sergeant Gale, a British soldier. It is a good visit, but he knows now that that part of his life is over.

On a visit to the Lytes, he is angry to see how differently Lavinia treats Isannah and Cilla, favoring one while scolding the other. Later, he learns that Mrs. Bessie, the Lytes' cook and housekeeper, is not a Tory like the Lytes, but a Patriot, and has been secretly working for Sam Adams. Mrs. Bessie tells him that the Sons of Liberty are planning to attack the Lytes at their summer place in Milton, a town outside of Boston.

Chapter 8: A World to Come

One night in August, Johnny sees the Lytes' coach rushing to the gates of Boston with a mob at its heels. Johnny learns that Mrs. Bessie warned the Lytes about the attack in time for them to escape, and he is glad that she was loyal to the family. Cilla remembers she has left the Lyte family silver in Milton and wants to get it before the mob steals it; Johnny goes with her. At the house, he finds an old Bible and learns that his mother was indeed a Lyte and had grown up in the Milton house. Cilla tells him to take his silver cup back, but he says that the past is not important anymore.

In the meantime, Rab is still trying to get a musket to use as a member of the Lexington militia. He arranges to buy one from a British soldier, but is betrayed and captured. However, the officer lets him go, calling him a boy. Johnny can't help but laugh when Rab tells him the story. Rab had always considered himself a man, and although relieved to escape punishment, he is insulted by the way he was dismissed.

Despite the political tensions, daily life goes on in Boston. Johnny continues to see Cilla regularly. She tells him that Madge married Sergeant Gale and the widowed Mrs. Lapham married Tweedie herself. He and Cilla remember the long-ago agreement that they would marry. Cilla states that Cilla Tremain has a fine ring to it. Johnny agrees.

The Observers meet again, and this time Johnny and Rab stay for the meeting. The Observers discuss setting up a spy network. Also at that meeting, Sam Adams says that he will not work for peace at the Continental Congress; it is too late for that. James Otis, the founder of the Observers, who had not been invited to this meeting because his behavior had become "queer" after a blow to the head, shows up anyway. He gives an impassioned speech about the rights of man and the far-reaching implications of the coming revolution, concluding that Americans will fight so that "a man can stand up."[54] Johnny lies awake at night thinking of Otis and his words.

Chapter 9: The Scarlet Deluge

With his connections at the Afric Queen, Johnny becomes part of the Patriots' spy network. They want to know when the British might march to the countryside to seize supplies being stockpiled for war. Paul Revere tells Johnny to stay "friends" with Dove because, as Colonel Smith's horse boy, Dove would probably know when something was going to happen. One day, when doing some work for Dove, Johnny meets Lieutenant Stranger again and the lieutenant says he can teach Johnny how to jump Goblin. They go to the Common that day and many others. Johnny is puzzled about British class distinctions; he is confused because Lieutenant Stranger treats him as an equal when they're riding, but as an inferior at all other times.

One day, on his way to delivering the *Boston Observer*, Johnny is on the Common. A British officer seizes the newspaper and orders Johnny to receive thirty lashes for sedition (inciting rebellion) because of the paper's Whig bias. The young private holding Goblin's reins is Pumpkin, whom Johnny knows from the Lytes' stable. Pumpkin mouths the word "spurs" and lets go of the bridle so that Johnny can get away. Johnny makes good his escape. Back at the Lytes' stable later that day, Pumpkin tells

By spying on the British, Johnny helped protect the Minutemen in the countryside who were making and stockpiling weapons.

Johnny he wants to desert and stay in the colonies. Johnny agrees to leave clothes for him and asks him to leave a musket for Rab. The clothes disappear and the musket is left, but Pumpkin never shows up to sneak out of Boston with Rab's uncle. Johnny assumes he got out another way.

It is now April 1775. Tension mounts as the Patriots wait for General Gage to make a move. One day, Johnny is on the Common exercising Colonel Smith's horses for Dove. He sees a deserter being led out to be shot and recognizes Pumpkin. He thinks about the eight muskets pointed at the young man, "eight cruel eyes,"[55] and does not know how anyone has the courage to face them. Pumpkin's death is frightening, and for the first time, Johnny doubts his own bravery in choosing to join the Patriot cause.

Chapter 10: "Disperse, Ye Rebels!"

On Saturday, April 15, Johnny brings news to Paul Revere and Joseph Warren that about seven hundred British troops have been alerted and soon will be on the march. Others, too, have noticed the activity. Revere rides out to Lexington to tell John Hancock and Sam Adams, who are staying there, that the British might be coming. He goes on to Concord to warn the Minutemen to hide ammunition and supplies stored there.

Johnny is angry when Rab leaves on Sunday to join the Minutemen in Lexington, especially since Rab doesn't seem to care that he's leaving Johnny. Johnny even offers to go with him, but Rab says Johnny is more useful as a spy in Boston. Johnny doesn't give Rab a proper good-bye and tries to catch him, but Rab is gone.

Two days later, April 18, Johnny listens to Dove complain at the Afric Queen stables. Piecing together different statements, he realizes the British will march that night and that Lexington and Concord are the likely targets. He rushes to tell Dr. Warren. Revere and another rider, Billy Dawes, prepare to spread the alarm. Johnny is sent to tell the sexton to hang two lanterns in Christ's Church as a signal that the British will be leaving Boston

Paul Revere rides through the night to warn that British troops are on the march.

by water. They will be transported across the Charles River rather than march out through the narrow neck of land that separates Boston from the countryside. Johnny later returns to Dr. Warren's and is sleeping soundly on the morning of April 19, when the first shots are fired at Lexington.

Chapter 11: Yankee Doodle

Johnny awakens to the sound of soldiers' marching. Dr. Warren tells him that fighting began in Lexington between the British and a small band of Minutemen. The doctor is leaving for Lexington. He is in danger of being arrested as a traitor in Boston, and his medical skills are needed in Lexington. The British scattered the Minutemen at Lexington, but hundreds or maybe thousands of militia are converging on Concord. Colonel Smith has sent for reinforcements. Dr. Warren asks Johnny to stay in Boston to see what he can learn and then to sneak out of the city in the confusion of the evening. Hearing that some men were killed at Lexington, Johnny worries about Rab.

Johnny joins the crowds milling about. The British flag goes by. Johnny thinks about all the liberties the flag has stood for and almost removes his hat in respect. Then he decides that it is too late. The meaning of liberty has expanded in the colonies and war has begun. As the British soldiers march along, he counts the regiments and wonders what chance the Minutemen, untrained and poorly armed, would have at Concord.

The British start arresting Patriots, but most have already fled the city. Johnny sends a message to Uncle Lorne. When he arrives at the print shop himself, he sees the sign is down and the door is smashed in. Aunt Jenifer is sitting alone sewing a large feather bed. The troops had come and gone. Suddenly, the bed moves and Uncle Lorne crawls out. Johnny tells them that from the disgusted looks he has seen on the faces of British officers, he believes the British are losing the fight with the colonial militias.

Johnny decides to disguise himself as a British soldier so he can get out of Boston. He stops by the Lytes' to get Pumpkin's old uniform. They are packing to return to England. Lavinia tells Johnny the whole story of his mother and father, but defends her father by saying they only put the pieces together recently. She also says her father will write out all the details and send them to Johnny so that when the war is over, he can put in a claim for property. Isannah chooses to go with Lavinia, but Cilla and Mrs. Bessie are staying to look after the house. Johnny arranges for Uncle Lorne and his family to move into the coach house so they will be safe and so that they can help Cilla and Mrs. Bessie. Over Mrs. Bessie's objections, he puts on Pumpkin's uniform. He says he has information for Dr. Warren and needs to find out if Rab is all right. Then he kisses Cilla good-bye and leaves. Wearing a British uniform, he suddenly wonders what happened to Madge's

Sergeant Gale, who had marched out to Lexington with the British troops.

Chapter 12: A Man Can Stand Up

Johnny heads for the ferry slip. He sees tired, dirty troops, many wounded, stepping off the boats from Charlestown. He notices that wounded officers are treated with greater respect than regular troops and thinks again of James Otis's words. Johnny also sees his friend Lieutenant Stranger wounded and wants to help him, but realizes he can't. They are at war. He finally gets a boat across by saying he has a message for the British lord Percy.

Once across, he takes off the British uniform. He hears news of Lexington and Concord. The Minutemen clashed with the British at the North Bridge in Concord and chased them back to Lexington. British reinforcements arrived, but so did more

Minutemen advance across a bridge at the Battle of Concord.

Minutemen. The British were driven back to Charlestown and the boats to Boston. Johnny tries to learn news of Rab, but no one knows of him.

Johnny can't travel farther until the next day. Finally, he hears that Dr. Warren is in Lexington. Along the way, he passes burned houses and sees a funeral procession. Finally at Lexington Green, Johnny finds Dr. Warren and learns that Rab has been mortally wounded. He is lying in Buckman's Tavern, just off the Green. Rab is weak and bleeding at the mouth. He tells Johnny he never even had a chance to fire his musket, but he was glad he had it. Johnny believes this is Rab's way of saying thank-you for getting him the musket. Rab also tells Johnny he can have the musket. Then he asks Johnny to check on his family at Silsbee Cove and gives Johnny a big smile. Johnny feels Rab's friendship and love in that smile.

No one is at Silsbee Cove, so Johnny feeds the animals and returns to Buckman's Tavern, where he learns that Rab has died. He realizes then that Rab sent him away so that he wouldn't be there to see his friend die. He and Dr. Warren remember James Otis's words and find meaning in Rab's death. Dr. Warren asks to see Johnny's hand and explains how the scar tissue caused the crippling. He says he can cut the thumb free if Johnny is brave enough. He makes no promises that Johnny can be a silversmith again, but says he will be able to shoot a gun. Waiting outside while the doctor prepares for the surgery, Johnny feels a true sense of belonging, that this is his country. Many men will die like Rab, but they give their lives so "that a man can stand up."

CHAPTER FOUR

The Cast of Characters

Johnny Tremain has a large cast of characters. Most are fictional, but some are real people from that period of history. When historical figures interact with fictional characters in novels, authors portray them in a way that is consistent with the historical record.

Sam Adams

Sam Adams is one of many historical figures who interact with the fictional Johnny Tremain. Adams was a major leader of the American Revolution and an early supporter of independence. He is important in *Johnny Tremain* because he is one of the leaders of the Observers.

Meeting Adams is also Johnny's first reward for being nice to someone. Instead of yelling at Adams's servant for accidentally dousing him with dishwater, as he normally would, Johnny says nothing. The servant apologizes and invites him in for some pie while she dries his clothes by the fire. In the kitchen

Samuel Adams was one of author Esther Forbes's ancestors.

sits Sam Adams himself. From then on, whenever Johnny delivers a message, Adams invites him in to talk.

Mrs. Bessie

Mrs. Bessie is the housekeeper and cook for the Lyte family. She is kind to Johnny when he visits Cilla there on Thursdays. Although Mrs. Bessie has worked for the Lytes for many years, she does not share their Tory views. She is a Patriot and has been secretly helping Sam Adams in his work for the Patriot cause.

Mrs. Bessie tells Johnny that the Sons of Liberty are planning to attack the Lytes at their summer place in Milton. Then, when the attack is imminent, she warns the family and they escape to Boston. Johnny likes her all the more for this act of loyalty to the family that has been good to her.

Dove

Dove is an apprentice in the Lapham household. Although two years older than Johnny, he is unskilled and lazy. He resents Johnny's favored place in the household and is angry when the younger boy orders him around and calls him names. It is Dove who hands Johnny the cracked crucible that spills the hot silver and cripples Johnny. Mr. Lapham says that Dove did not intend to harm Johnny, only to embarrass him. Dove shows no sympathy for Johnny's disability, however, and enjoys giving him orders and making fun of him.

Dove appears again at the Boston Tea Party, when he tries to steal some tea. Eventually, he is fired from the Lapham household by Mr. Tweedie. Later, he shows up in the stable at the Afric Queen as horse boy for Colonel Smith, a British officer. While Dove works for the British, Johnny stays close to him, hoping to learn something about what the British army is planning. Luckily, Dove's complaining gives Johnny enough information to realize that the British will be marching to Lexington and Concord on the night of April 18.

John Hancock

John Hancock is another historical figure who appears in the novel. He is a wealthy Boston merchant, and as the novel begins, he orders a silver sugar bowl from Johnny's master, Mr. Lapham. The sugar bowl is to replace the ruined one of a favorite tea set belonging to Hancock's aunt. Because the sugar bowl is to be a birthday gift for the aunt, it must be delivered before seven the following Monday morning. Johnny burns his hand while attempting to meet this deadline.

John Hancock's signature is one of many gracing the Declaration of Independence.

In his unsuccessful search for work after the accident, Johnny goes to Hancock to see if he can apprentice himself as a clerk. However, when he can't write with his crippled hand, Hancock sends him away. The merchant then sends a servant after Johnny to give him a bag of silver coins. Hancock appears later as a member of the Observers, but he does not interact with Johnny.

Mr. Lapham

Johnny's elderly master was at one time a talented silversmith. In fact, he made a tea set for John Hancock's uncle, which is why Hancock comes to his shop to have the new sugar bowl made. However, Lapham is now more interested in reading the Bible than he is in being a silversmith and leaves much of the work to his apprentices. When he gathers the family for prayer, he often chooses biblical passages about pride for Johnny to read. He foreshadows Johnny's accident by saying, "You're getting above yourself. . . . God is going to send you a dire punishment for your pride."[56]

Both Johnny Tremain and Mr. Lapham were fictional characters in a fictional story woven into the actual history of the American Revolution.

After Johnny's injury, Lapham shows himself to be a kindly man. While he tells Johnny that he must look for a new profession, he assures him that he has a home with the Laphams as long as he needs it. He also tells Johnny that Dove handed him the cracked crucible on purpose and asks Johnny to forgive the other boy.

Isannah Lapham

Isannah is the youngest of the four Lapham daughters. She is eight years old when the novel opens. She is beautiful, but also sickly, "hardly worth the bother she was to raise,"[57] according to her mother. But fourteen-year-old Cilla loves her and takes care of her. Both Cilla and Isannah are favorites of Johnny, and the three young people often tease each other playfully.

Isannah's sickly nature is important because her inability to sleep is the reason Johnny, Cilla, and Isannah are sitting at the end of the wharf one hot night in July. That night, Johnny tells Cilla about his relationship to the Lytes and shows her his silver cup. Later, at Johnny's trial for theft, Cilla can testify that she saw the cup before the date Jonathan Lyte reported it stolen. Even though Isannah is asleep and never sees the cup, with Rab's coaching she rushes into Johnny's trial and backs up Cilla's story about seeing the cup.

Isannah, however, is a spoiled little girl, enjoying the attention her beauty brings. When Lavinia Lyte is taken with Isannah's beauty and offers to raise her, the child is eager to accept provided Cilla can come along. Lavinia agrees and then pampers Isannah, while treating Cilla as a servant. Isannah loves the attention and fails to notice how Cilla is mistreated. She adapts too well to the comforts of her new lifestyle. At the end of the novel, when the Revolution begins, Isannah chooses the luxuries and excitement Lavinia can offer her over Cilla's simple love, and she decides to go to England with the Lytes.

Mrs. Lapham

Mrs. Lapham is Mr. Lapham's widowed daughter-in-law. She is outspoken and has no time for social graces. She works hard, constantly worrying about feeding her large household. Knowing that any income can help the family, it is she who gives Johnny permission to work on the Sabbath, the day he burns his hand.

Once Johnny can no longer work, Mrs. Lapham abandons him as useless. She turns against him completely when he is rude to Mr. Tweedie, the silversmith she brings in to help her father-in-law run the shop. Later in the novel, as Johnny matures, he understands Mrs. Lapham better, and realizes how hard she worked to keep food on the table.

Priscilla (Cilla) Lapham

Cilla is the second youngest of the Lapham girls. She is Johnny's age, fourteen, when the novel begins. It is supposed that she and Johnny will marry someday and inherit the silversmith's shop, although neither one dwells on the idea. Cilla likes and respects Johnny, and despite the teasing back and forth, he feels the same way about her. She is a bright girl who loves to draw and is learning to read. She is also fiercely protective of her little sister, Isannah.

Cilla remains Johnny's friend through all of his troubles, even after her mother declares that all marriage plans are off. When Johnny is on trial for theft, Cilla defies her mother and testifies in his behalf. She later meets him regularly, giving him news of his old home.

When Cilla and Isannah go to live with Lavinia Lyte, Cilla is treated as a servant, while Isannah becomes the pampered child. Since she has always loved Isannah, Cilla doesn't complain about

Cilla (seated) is Johnny's age and her family assumes that she and Johnny will marry someday.

her treatment. She even shows herself to be responsible and loyal to the Lytes when the family is forced to abandon their summer home by an angry mob. It is Cilla who insists on returning to retrieve the family silver she had forgotten to pack. In the end, too, she accepts the fact that she has lost Isannah to Lavinia and doesn't try to bribe the younger girl to stay with her. Cilla, however, remains in Boston with Mrs. Bessie to look after the Lytes' house.

Mr. Lorne

Rab's Uncle Lorne is a printer and publisher of the Patriot newspaper, the *Boston Observer*. He is described as a timid man, yet he is a member of the Observers and is not afraid to publish what the British call treasonous material. On Rab's recommendation, he hires Johnny to deliver his newspaper on horseback. He and his wife Jenifer show Johnny what a loving family can be. They welcome him into their home and treat him like family. When he has free time, Johnny is trusted to look after their infant son, and they allow him the precious luxury of reading books in their library.

At the end of the story, angry British soldiers destroy Uncle Lorne's print shop. He escapes capture, though, by hiding in the feather bed his wife is repairing. Johnny then arranges for him and his family to move to the Lytes' household after the Lytes leave for England. Away from the print shop, they will be hidden and safe, and they can help Mrs. Bessie and Cilla take care of the stable and house.

Lavinia Lyte

Lavinia is the daughter of the wealthy merchant Jonathan Lyte. Her beauty fascinates Johnny, yet he imagines her to be arrogant, disagreeable, and bad-tempered. After her father spurns Johnny and has him brought to trial for stealing, Johnny sees little of Lavinia. Only when Cilla and Isannah are taken in by the Lytes does Johnny sees Lavinia regularly. Then he is angry with her because she treats the two girls differently—Isannah becomes a pampered pet, Cilla is treated as a servant.

While Lavinia is indeed often spoiled and bad-tempered, she is a devoted daughter who takes good care of her ailing father. She also tries to make amends with Johnny. Before leaving for England, where she is to marry a wealthy nobleman, she tells Johnny about his past and his relationship to the Lyte family. She promises that her father will put the facts about Johnny in writing and send them to him, so that when the war is over, he can put in a claim for property.

Jonathan Lyte

Jonathan Lyte is a wealthy Boston merchant, father of Lavinia Lyte and uncle of Johnny's deceased mother (although neither Johnny nor Lyte know the nature of their relationship until the end of the book). He is a Tory and loyal to the king, although Rab maintains that he voices support to both sides and then does what he can to make money.

Lyte is shrewd, but he is also dishonest. He tricks Johnny into bringing his cup to his house and then has him arrested for stealing. At Johnny's trial, he lies about how many silver cups existed—saying four were made, when the truth was five. He also tries to bribe the Laphams into keeping Cilla from testifying on Johnny's behalf. Later, he takes Johnny's cup and tries to have Johnny kidnapped to sea.

When the war begins, Lyte returns to England with Lavinia. He is in bad health and would probably not survive a civil war. In England, he will be well cared for, as Lavinia is engaged to marry a nobleman.

James Otis

The historical James Otis, born in 1725, was a staunch Patriot and noted speaker. In his later years, he became insane, some believe as a result of a blow to his head that he received in 1769. He appears in only two scenes in *Johnny Tremain*, and is referred

to as having "grown so queer, the other members [of the Observers] did not wish him about, even in his lucid periods."[58]

But Otis is an important character because his speech to the Observers encapsulates the main theme of the book—that the American Revolution was fought for the rights of all men, so "that a man can stand up." Johnny is inspired by Otis's words and keeps coming back to them, especially at the end of the book when he tries to find some meaning in Rab's death.

James Otis inspires Johnny with his speech to the Observers.

Pumpkin

Pumpkin is a British soldier who makes extra money as a groom for the Lytes. Although he appears in only a few pages in the book, he plays an important role in Johnny's development. Johnny first meets Pumpkin at the Lytes' home when he visits Cilla. Whereas Cilla has always been "just Cilla" to Johnny, Pumpkin treats her like a lady, opening doors for her and bowing politely. This makes Johnny jealous and makes him see how he has taken Cilla for granted.

Later, Pumpkin helps Johnny escape a flogging from a British officer. When they meet again at the Lytes', Pumpkin tells Johnny that he wants to desert the army and stay in the colonies. "I want to live here forever," he says. "A farm of my own. Cows. Poor folk can't get things like that over in England."[59] Johnny gives him clothes to wear and arranges safe passage out of Boston with one of Rab's uncles. But Pumpkin is captured and Johnny sees him shot by a firing squad. Not only does Johnny feel pity for the young man, but for one brief moment, he is grateful that his crippled hand will keep him out of combat. He will never have to face the muskets of battle staring at him. These fearful thoughts cause him to question his own courage for the first time. With Pumpkin's death, then, the cocky Johnny grows up a little more.

Paul Revere

The historical Paul Revere is best remembered for his famous ride to Lexington and Concord the night of April 18, 1775—

Paul Revere helped organize the Boston Tea Party.

and he makes that ride in *Johnny Tremain*. However, Johnny knows him long before as a master silversmith and goes to him for advice on making John Hancock's sugar bowl. At that time, Revere offers to buy out Johnny's contract with Mr. Lapham and take him as his own apprentice, but Johnny refuses, saying that the Laphams depend on him.

After Johnny's injury and new life with Rab, Revere appears as an inspiring leader of the Observers. Revere helps organize the Boston Tea Party; he is an important rider for the Patriots, and takes Johnny into his confidence. Johnny delivers messages to him and for him, and becomes one of his spies.

Rab Silsbee

Rab is a printer's apprentice who works for his Uncle Lorne. He is two years older than Johnny. Johnny looks up to Rab and considers him to be his best friend. When they first meet, Johnny is hungry and desperately looking for work. Rab offers him food and a friendly ear. He also offers Johnny a job, and later brings help when Johnny is arrested for stealing Lyte's silver cup.

When the two boys live together in the loft above the print shop, Rab's simple observations and comments start Johnny on the path to growing up. For example, Rab's casual comment on Johnny's quick temper, asking if it is fun to go around insulting people, causes Johnny to think about how he acts and what he says. Associating with Rab also brings Johnny into the turbulent politics engulfing Boston. Rab is a Patriot, and Johnny listens to his opinions. Since the Observers meet in Johnny and Rab's loft, Johnny learns about them and is eventually trusted with some of their secrets. Rab trusts him from the beginning and Johnny wants to be worthy of that trust.

Yet Rab himself remains a puzzle throughout the book. He is seen through Johnny's eyes, so the reader never knows what he is thinking or feeling. He comes from a large family in Lexington and seems to have grown up surrounded by love. Apprenticed to his uncle, he is easygoing and comfortable with his life. He seems interested in other people (when Johnny first meets Rab, the young printer is listening intently to a woman talking about her lost pig) and sensitive to their needs.

Like most people, however, Rab can be contradictory. He is usually quiet and relaxed, but when aroused, he can be a strong fighter. And he is uncaring of Johnny's feelings when he heads off to Lexington so eagerly. He dismisses Johnny's offer to go with him and never says he'll miss his friend. In a rare glimpse at Rab's point of view, Forbes writes that he "was going to fight—and the thought made some dark part of him happy."[60]

After the fighting begins, Rab becomes the focus of Johnny's worry when he hears that some men were killed at Lexington. At the end of the novel, as Rab lies dying, Johnny feels only misery and concern for his friend. Johnny thinks that he never knew the real Rab. But then, when Rab smiles at him, Johnny believes in Rab's love for him. For Johnny, "Everything he had never put in words was in that smile."[61]

Rab's death at the end of the book is inevitable. James Otis foreshadows it when he looks at the young man and says that some people will give their lives in the struggle for freedom. Rab's death is also necessary to show Johnny and the reader that liberty is not freely given, but must be won with sacrifice.

Lieutenant Stranger

A fictional British officer, Stranger is an aide to the historical Colonel Smith. Although Forbes doesn't comment on it, his name seems to be no accident. He is a stranger to the colonies and in many ways he remains a stranger to Johnny, even though they often ride together.

Lieutenant Stranger is described as a young man whose looks and manner remind Johnny of Rab, so it is clear that Forbes intended him to be a sympathetic character. When he and Johnny first meet, the lieutenant wants to commandeer Johnny's horse Goblin for Colonel Smith. Knowing how skittish the horse is, Johnny flaps a sheet at him when Lieutenant Stranger tries to ride him. Naturally, the horse rears and Lieutenant Stranger flies off. The young officer takes it with good humor, and even offers to teach Johnny how to jump with the horse.

Johnny becomes friends with the young officer, and feels admiration approaching worship for his skill with horses. Their friendship, however, also introduces Johnny to the strong British sense of social class. Lieutenant Stranger is a British officer and a gentleman. Although he treats Johnny as an equal when they are riding together, once they are back at the stables and off their horses, he treats Johnny as an inferior. Johnny has not been exposed to such class consciousness before and it puzzles him. These attitudes, however, do not stop Johnny from liking the officer. Near the end of the book, Johnny sees a wounded Lieutenant Stranger returning from Lexington and Concord and instinctively moves to help him. He stops only when he realizes they are now on opposite sides of a war. Dressed in Pumpkin's old uniform and planning to sneak over to Charlestown to join the Patriots, he would endanger his own life by revealing himself. A mature Johnny thinks of how war changes everything.

Johnny was portrayed by Hal Stalmaster in the Disney movie Johnny Tremain.

Johnny Tremain

The title character, Johnny Tremain is a talented, fourteen-year-old silversmith's apprentice when the book opens. The entire household of his master, Mr. Lapham, depends on him to keep the silversmith business going—and he knows it. This makes the young teenager arrogant, and he often disregards the feelings of others. But Johnny's selfish, cocky attitude is transformed as the novel progresses. He faces tragedy and death and learns to be part of a larger cause as he moves toward adulthood.

The novel traces Johnny's growth over a two-year period, from July 1773 to April 1775. An accident with molten silver cripples Johnny's right hand and leaves him without work. This, the first tragedy he must face, deflates his ego and leaves him despondent. But he has the good fortune to meet printer's apprentice Rab Silsbee and eventually accepts Rab's job offer to deliver the *Boston Observer*, a Patriot newspaper. From then on, both his outer and inner worlds expand. He sees new sights with his rides into the countryside, and Rab introduces him to the world of politics. Soon Johnny, who had been exposed to little besides his craft and religion at the Laphams', becomes a fervent Patriot. By observing Rab and heeding his comments, Johnny slowly starts to change his behavior, too. He learns to be patient and considerate, and most importantly, he learns to look beyond his own needs to participate in the struggle for national liberty.

His new awareness of others and the Patriot cause helps Johnny understand the meaning of James Otis's impassioned speech about the "rights of man" and the idea of fighting so that "a man can stand up." He sees the horror of Pumpkin's execution for desertion, knowing that all the young soldier wanted was a little piece of land to call his own. He becomes aware of the rigidity of the British social class through his friendship with Lieutenant Stranger. He watches the bedraggled British army return to Boston and notices that the wounded privates are tossed roughly from the boats. He thinks, "It is just as James Otis said. We are fighting, partly, for just that. Because a man is a private is no reason he should be treated like cordwood."[62]

At the end of the book, Johnny is sixteen and a young man, ready to assume adult responsibilities. When he loses his friend, he learns to accept death. With Dr. Warren's help, he can even find some meaning in Rab's death, believing that he died for a cause that was right. Johnny's new maturity also allows him to realize that his wounded hand is just a wounded hand, not something to be ashamed of. When Dr. Warren asks again to look at it, he complies. As the novel ends, Johnny is waiting for Dr. Warren to operate on his hand to restore some movement to it. Johnny will then take up Rab's musket and continue the fight. Like Rab and thousands of others, he will risk his life for an important ideal, "that a man can stand up." He is ready to fight for a better world.

Dr. Joseph Warren

Another historical figure, Warren was a respected physician and Patriot who was killed in 1775 at the Battle of Bunker Hill. In the novel, he is a member of the Observers and a friend of Paul Revere and Sam Adams. His name is first mentioned when Mrs. Lapham

Dr. Joseph Warren was a real person who was killed at the Battle of Bunker Hill in 1775.

decides *not* to call him to treat Johnny's burned hand, a decision that has fateful consequences, as it leaves Johnny's hand crippled and forces him to leave the small world of the silversmith shop.

Warren is presented as a good, caring physician who treats all the sick, Patriot and Tory alike. Even Lavinia Lyte calls him when her father is sick. Johnny meets Warren when he carries messages to the Observers. Warren sees Johnny's crippled hand and asks to have a closer look, but at that time Johnny is too proud and embarrassed to let him.

Just as he did in history, Warren plays an important role in Patriot activities in the novel. He confers with Paul Revere about warning Lexington and Concord that British troops are coming. When he leaves Boston on April 19, he asks Johnny to stay in Boston for the day to see what he can learn. His confidence in Johnny and Johnny's acceptance of the responsibility is a clear sign of Johnny's maturity.

When Johnny meets Warren again in Lexington, it is the doctor who tells him that Rab is dying. Acting like the father that Johnny never knew, Warren helps him find meaning in Rab's death by reminding him of James Otis's words that some men will die for the cause of freedom. Warren then again asks to examine Johnny's hand. This time, the grown-up Johnny allows him to and learns that surgery may restore some movement to his hand. The novel ends as Warren readies his instruments to begin the operation.

Minor Characters

Minor characters are not as well developed as the major ones—and some appear very briefly—but they are necessary to add depth and reality to a novel. In *Johnny Tremain*, the minor characters fill out Johnny's world, sometimes exposing him to the best and worst in human nature.

John Adams

The real John Adams played an important role in the American Revolution and in the fledgling United States. He was a lawyer and an advocate of American independence. In *Johnny Tremain*, however, John Adams appears only briefly as a member of the Observers. Johnny sees him talking to Dr. Warren at one meeting, and at another meeting, sees him discussing the upcoming Continental Congress with Sam Adams.

Dr. Ben Church

Another historical figure, Church is a member of the Observers. Johnny doesn't trust him and he suspects that Paul Revere and Dr. Warren don't trust him either. On April 15, 1775, when Revere is leaving Boston to ride to Lexington, he refuses to answer

John Adams became the second president of the United States.

Dr. Church's questions about what is happening. Johnny hears Revere mutter about Church, "But I can't trust that fellow . . . never have, never will."[63]

The real Church was indeed a spy for the British, posing as a member of the Sons of Liberty. He was found out by George Washington in the summer of 1775 when he tried to smuggle a coded letter to the British out of Patriot-controlled Boston. Washington wanted him hanged, but the laws of Congress would not allow it at that time. Instead, Church was imprisoned in Connecticut.

Billy Dawes

Another historical figure, Dawes was another rider who warned Lexington and Concord that the British were coming the night of April 18, 1775. While Paul Revere rowed across the river to Charlestown, Dawes left Boston across the narrow strip of land

Billy Dawes was a real person and, like Paul Revere, rode on horseback across the countryside warning of the approaching British.

called the Boston Neck. One account says that he got by the British guards by dressing as a countryman going on a journey. In *Johnny Tremain*, Dawes is chosen to ride because he is a good actor. Johnny watches Dawes and his wife put together his disguise as a drunken farmer. He is impressed by the bravery of both Dawes and his wife.

Sergeant Gale

Gale is a British marine sergeant whom Madge Lapham falls in love with and eventually marries. He is polite to Johnny, and Johnny likes him right away. Johnny sees Gale and Madge when the sergeant is getting ready to march to Lexington on April 19, along with other British reinforcements. Johnny's ability to see people as individuals rather than "enemy" is evident when he comforts Madge, who is in tears at her husband's departure. The reader never learns what happens to Sergeant Gale in the battle.

Gran' Hopper

Hopper is the midwife Mrs. Lapham calls in to treat Johnny's burned hand. Although the old woman is skilled in her use of painkillers, she binds up the hand with the thumb bent over the palm instead of making sure the healing hand is kept flat. As a result, scar tissue attaches Johnny's thumb to his palm and his hand becomes useless for any fine work.

Dorcas Lapham

Dorcas is the middle daughter in the Lapham household, sixteen years old when the book opens. Although plump and strong like her mother and older sister, she longs for elegance. Johnny doesn't like her at the beginning of the book, but later, when she marries Frizel, Junior, a leather dresser, he feels pity for her that she'll never have the elegance she craves.

Madge Lapham

The oldest of the Lapham daughters, Madge is eighteen when the novel opens. Johnny admits that she is a hard worker, but he still doesn't like her. Later, however, when he sees her in love with British marine sergeant Gale, he acknowledges that she can be agreeable. After Dorcas elopes, Madge is supposed to marry Mr. Tweedie. Instead, she runs off and marries Sergeant Gale. At the end of the book, Johnny comforts her when her new husband must march off to Lexington with his regiment.

Mrs. Jenifer Lorne

Mrs. Lorne is Rab's aunt and Uncle Lorne's wife. Although a minor character, she performs two important functions in the novel. First, she gives Johnny love and acceptance. Second, near the end of the book, Mrs. Lorne shows her courage and saves her husband from the British soldiers. When they come looking for him, she hides him inside a feather bed she is sewing—and sits calmly stitching as the British soldiers destroy the print shop.

Lydia

Lydia is the African American laundress at the Afric Queen. She doesn't like the British officers who are staying at the inn and so helps Johnny on two occasions. First, she helps him "spook" Goblin and so prevent Lieutenant Stranger from commandeering the horse for Colonel Smith. Second, she gives Johnny pieces of a note written by Lieutenant Stranger. Johnny, Rab, and Uncle Lorne put the pieces together and learn about a planned British march.

Dusty Miller

Miller is the third apprentice in the Lapham household. Younger than Johnny, he doesn't resent Johnny's authority as much as Dove does. After Johnny's accident, Dusty slowly fades from the story, with Cilla finally saying that he has run away to sea.

Josiah Quincy had a son (pictured) also named Josiah who also became a lawyer. Josiah Jr. would go on to serve as a member of the House of Representatives, president of Harvard University, and mayor of Boston.

Josiah Quincy

Quincy was a real person, an outstanding lawyer who worked with John Adams. He also wrote many essays and articles on the Patriot cause. In 1774, he was sent to England to argue for the colonists and died in 1775 on the return trip. In *Johnny Tremain*, he is a member of the Observers, and more important, is Johnny's defense lawyer. He takes Johnny's case for free, visits him in jail, and supports him throughout the trial.

Percival Tweedie

Tweedie is the silversmith whom Mrs. Lapham brings to the shop after Johnny is injured. He is a timid man and, seen through Johnny's eyes, a comic one as well. When Johnny insults Tweedie and calls him a "squeak-pig,"[64] Tweedie becomes his enemy. Tweedie later joins Mrs. Lapham in trying to prevent Cilla from testifying for Johnny at his trial. Mrs. Lapham is determined that Mr. Tweedie marry one of her daughters to ensure that the silversmith business remains in the family. When the two older girls elope, Mrs. Lapham marries him herself.

CHAPTER FIVE

Critical Analysis

J ohnny Tremain was an instant critical success when it was
published in 1943, receiving almost universal praise for its
historic realism and believable characters. Some later critics—
viewing history and war with a more skeptical eye—have been
less admiring. They have criticized the book's glorification of war
and its unquestioning support of the Patriot view. Still, the
majority find much to praise in the book, and it has remained on
lists of "best books" for young people throughout the years.
Despite its obvious bias toward the Patriot cause, most critics see
the novel as an excellent example of historical fiction and com-
mend its uplifting theme of the "rights of man." They also see it,
first and foremost, as a novel of character.

Coming of Age

Literary criticism holds that most great novels have a main character who changes and grows as a result of what happens to him
or her. This is especially true in novels for young people, in which
growing up and finding a place in the world are important
themes. *Johnny Tremain* offers a clear example, as it follows
Johnny's life from age fourteen through sixteen, watching him
struggle with loss and the building of a new future.

Dwight L. Burton, author of *Literature Study in the High
Schools*, calls Johnny "one of the most interesting characters in junior
fiction. At the outset of the story he is the completely vain and cock-

sure young bully. An injury to his hand ends his career as a silver-smith's apprentice, completely changes his life, and involves him ultimately in the revolutionary movement."[65] Another critic, M. Sarah Smedman, also discusses the importance of Johnny as a char-acter: "The success of *Johnny*, as of all memorable fiction, derives primarily from the vitality of its protagonist and the authenticity of his development."[66] Smedman sees Johnny's growing maturity as realistic and credible, as his friendship with Rab and involvement in the coming Revolution force him to look at the world outside of his own self-interest.

Johnny appears to be credible because he is far from perfect, and most teens can identify with his feelings, first of pride, then of humiliation. Proud of his skills, he scorns fellow apprentice Dove for his clumsiness and calls him "the stupidest animal God ever made."[67] Although pious Mr. Lapham tries to make Johnny see the inherent worth of all people, most teens probably feel closer to Johnny's impatience and pride. Unfortunately, this

Johnny's view of the world changes as a result of his relationships and the war raging around him.

arrogance brings about his downfall. Brimming with resentment, Dove deliberately hands him the cracked crucible that results in the injury.

In the few seconds that it takes his hand to burn, Johnny loses everything: his talent, his place in the household, his confidence, his future. Ashamed of his hand, confused about what to do, he keeps his hand in his pocket and roams the streets. He begins looking for other work, but looks down on some occupations, such as soap boiling or rope making, and cannot imagine himself in others, such as butchering. Even when he meets Rab and is offered a job as a delivery boy, he initially says no. His pride insists he can return only when he has achieved success doing work he likes. When everything else fails, Johnny tries to use his relationship to the Lyte family as an easy solution to getting back on his feet, but there he finds only treachery and almost ends up on the gallows. Finally, after escaping Lyte's clutches for the second time, he swallows his pride and accepts Rab's offer.

The friendship, love, and acceptance he finds with Rab and his family help Johnny look at the world and himself in a different way. Rab becomes a role model, never criticizing, but asking questions, such as "Was it fun . . . going about letting everybody who got in your way have it?"[68] For the first time in his life, Johnny starts to think about other people's feelings. Through Rab, he also becomes involved in Patriot activities and soon embraces their cause, carrying messages for the secret Observers and participating in the Boston Tea Party. The tumultuous months go by, and Johnny continues to change and grow.

The deepening conflict between the Patriots and the British hastens Johnny's growth, as he is forced to face serious social and political issues. Smedman discusses Johnny's path to maturity:

> As Johnny renders significant service to the patriots, he is taken more into their confidence, understands their cause, and espouses their values. Simultaneously he becomes less

Friendship and acceptance from Rab and Rab's family foster Johnny's growing maturity.

self-centered, more concerned for his friends and for the general welfare of all people. Fickle when he is caught up in his new life, he forgets about the Laphams, though never quite about Cilla; he discovers and finds it less difficult to display his real feelings for her as Rab and Pumpkin pay her attention. Johnny's spirit expands as he grows happier, more confident of his own place in his new world. His tight-fisted self-concern relaxes. As he comes to know others as individuals rather than merely as satellites of himself, he begins to acquire sympathy for them: not only for the Whigs, but also for the British soldiers.[69]

Johnny finds sympathy, too, for a Tory who is chased and beaten by a group of Sons of Liberty for taking down one of their posters—and he admires the man's defiant courage. He comes to realize how hard Mrs. Lapham, whom he had scorned during his days as an apprentice, worked to keep food on her family's table. Once he resented her bellowing voice in the morning. Now, for the first time, he thinks that perhaps she too would rather have stayed in bed on a cold winter morning. Johnny's feelings for Dove change, too. His anger and bitterness fade as he feels loved and accepted. Although he never likes Dove—the older boy's laziness, irresponsibility, and self-pitying attitude make him truly unlikable—Johnny is able to feel pity for him when Mr. Tweedie fires him and he ends up working at the stables where the other stable boys make fun of him.

But there is more to come as hostilities between the Patriots and British increase. When Johnny sees Pumpkin killed by a firing squad for desertion, he is frightened and doubts his own courage. "Was the 'bold Johnny Tremain' really a coward at heart?"[70] he asks himself. This, too, helps him grow. As Smedman says, Johnny's strong reaction to James Otis's idealism about the rights of man is "natural [and] inevitable. . . . Johnny's selflessness is now credible, his independence and courage, always admirable, now truer because he has learned to doubt his own superiority."[71]

In the end, Johnny is able to face the loss of his best friend, Rab, and take up the fight with Rab's own gun. He tells Mrs. Bessie, who asks whether sixteen is a boy or a man, "A boy in time of peace and a man in time of war."[72] It is wartime and Johnny Tremain has become a man.

Johnny's Growth Reflects the Nation's Rite of Passage

Some critics have also seen Johnny as a symbol of the Revolution, citing parallels between his growth and that of the colonies. Elyse Trevers writes in *Beacham's Guide to Literature for Young Adults*, "Just as Johnny strives to become an independent adult, the Boston Whigs struggle to win independence for their land."[73] She notes, too, that just as Johnny becomes an adult at the end of the novel, the colonists are on their way toward winning their independence.

Michael Kammen devotes an entire chapter of his book *A Season of Youth* to the idea of "The American Revolution as National *Rite de Passage*." He defines "rite of passage" as the rite, or ritual, a person or culture goes through while moving from one stage of development to another. A rite of passage, he explains, has three distinct phases: separation from the familiar, a period of transition during which the past is gone but the future is still uncertain, and finally reintegration, that is, the individual becomes part of a new structure or organization with new rights and responsibilities.

Many American literary works deal with a young person's rite of passage from youth to adulthood. Among several Kammen mentions are two about the American Revolution that are still popular today, *April Morning* by Howard Fast and *My Brother Sam Is Dead* by James Lincoln Collier and Christopher Collier. But he focuses on *Johnny Tremain*, calling it "a personalization of Revolutionary Boston and its inevitable destiny. . . . Its plot, quite simply, is an epitome of the American Revolution as *rite de passage*."[74]

Johnny is fourteen, Kammen notes, when the book opens, his future secure. Then everything changes when he burns his hand. His old world is gone, and he goes through a time of confusion and indecision. But he eventually finds a place for himself in a new order. Later, secure in his new life, Johnny returns to the Laphams and sees the "birth and death" room where he lay after the accident. He thinks that "in a way he had died in that room; at least something had happened and the bright little silversmith's apprentice was no more. He stood here again at the threshold, but now he was somebody else."[75]

In the same way, says Kammen, popular American culture views the Revolution as a rite of passage from dependence on England to independence, with an emphasis on America as the

Many Americans consider the American Revolution as a rite of passage from dependence to independence.

land of youth. He quotes Thomas Paine, who asks in *Common Sense*, "Is it the interest of a man to be a boy all his life?" and Loyalist Samuel Seabury, who writes, "You will find [Great Britain] a vigorous matron, just approaching a green old age; and with spirit and strength sufficient to chastise her undutiful and rebellious children. . . . But we are rushing into a war with our parent state without offering the least concession."[76]

Kammen further notes that Johnny's problems and symbolic rebirth from 1773 to 1775 parallel those of the colonies as they move toward Lexington and ultimately a new order. He also points to the end of the book, where Johnny has become not only a man, but a "morally superior young American."[77] Johnny stands on the Lexington Green and looks to a greater future:

"True, Rab had died. Hundreds would die, but not the thing they died for. 'A man can stand up . . .'"[78]

The Importance of the Common Man

Whether Esther Forbes consciously thought of Johnny as a symbol of the Revolution is unknown, but it is clear that she was interested in the role of ordinary people in the Revolution. She was intrigued by the lives of apprentices and saw Paul Revere as representing the "average man." Without the efforts of hundreds of other average men, she said, there would have been no Revolution. Johnny himself was intended to be "a human, normal boy, not too good, occasionally mischievous and downright bad."[79]

This focus has been noted by others. Rosemary K. Coffey and Elizabeth F. Howard write in *America as Story* that the "Boston Tea Party and the battles of Lexington and Concord are portrayed from the viewpoints of ordinary people involved in the events."[80] Lois R. Kuznets, too, says in her article for *American Women Writers* that the novel shows Forbes's "intense interest in the part that individuals, significant or insignificant, play in historical events."[81]

If Johnny and many other characters are ordinary, however, they rise to extraordinary heights when events call for it. Smedman writes that "Forbes' artistic aim in depicting an historical crisis seems to have been to portray human greatness, liberated in its ordinary as well as its important representatives."[82] There are many examples in the novel, beginning with Johnny's growing awareness of a cause outside of himself. He uses his wits to obtain valuable information from Dove, then evades British troops, makes his way across the river to Charlestown, and arrives in Lexington in time to say good-bye to his dying friend.

Many characters risk—and some lose—their lives in the struggle. Rab is a key example. In simpler times, he would have been a printer like his uncle. With the coming Revolution, however, he joins the Minutemen and gives his life at Lexington. Average people are rising to the demands of extraordinary times.

Human greatness is seen on the British side, too. Pumpkin risks his life in an effort to be free and is executed as a deserter, while Madge's husband Sergeant Gale, loyal to the king, is presented as a man of courage with a sense of duty.

Other characters, ordinary people, also rise to the occasion. Uncle Lorne, who is repeatedly described as a timid man, publishes a radical Patriot newspaper, is a member of the Observers, and even allows the group to meet in the loft above his print shop. When the British soldiers are coming, the frightened man tells his wife he is not afraid to die. Fortunately, she, too, uses her wits to act quickly. She hides him in the feather bed she is sewing and remains steadfast while the soldiers storm through their shop.

Many commoners accomplish smaller but no less important feats. Unknown apprentices carry out the work at the Boston Tea Party. Mrs. Bessie is a simple housekeeper, but she tells Johnny that she has been secretly helping Sam Adams for years. Lydia, the African American laundress at the Afric Queen, spies for Johnny and gives him important information taken from Lieutenant Stranger's wastebasket. Cilla not only defies her mother and testifies at Johnny's trial, but like Johnny, she assumes adult responsibilities at sixteen. She has the maturity to let her beloved sister go while she stays with Mrs. Bessie to take care of the Lyte home in Boston.

A major theme of Johnny Tremain *is that ordinary people, like this Minuteman, can play important roles in history.*

Through *Johnny Tremain*, Forbes truly shows readers that ordinary people play important roles in history.

Johnny Tremain as a Historical Novel

The history that Forbes presents is consistently called "alive." The authors of *A Critical History of Children's Literature* say, "So alive is Johnny, so real is Boston of Revolutionary times, that it is difficult to believe that Esther Forbes has 'made up' anything at all. Here is absolute truth. . . . John Hancock, Sam Adams, Josiah Quincy, Paul Revere are no longer mere names in a history lesson. They are living people, with all the faults and failings of humans."[83]

The *Saturday Review of Literature* concurred, saying in its 1943 review that Forbes "takes us, with Johnny, to the secret meetings of the Sons of Liberty. . . . We hear and see Samuel Adams and John Hancock and Paul Revere. . . . [We see] Aunt Jenifer calmly sewing on a feather bed while a British officer searches the house and her husband lies, nearly smothered, under it at her feet. . . . Always, the people *live* as people do live under the pressure of great events."[84]

With such a realistic presentation of a world in turmoil, *Johnny Tremain* fits the classic definition of a historical novel. According to C. Hugh Holman's *A Handbook to Literature*, this classic formula holds that a historical novel seriously reconstructs a period of history in which "two cultures are in conflict, one dying and the other being born; into this cultural conflict, fictional personages are introduced who participate in actual historical events and move among actual personages from history."[85] These fictional characters personalize the impact of historical events and allow readers to see how such events affected the people living through them.

Writing specifically about literature for young people, Linda Levstik says that historical fiction can create a sense of history so powerful that young people can actually experience in their imagination the joys and sufferings of those in another time.

With its presentation of history through the eyes of a sympathetic and realistic adolescent, *Johnny Tremain* is often cited as a book that meets that demanding criteria.

Although Johnny is fictional, real events like the Boston Tea Party, the execution of a deserter, and the confusion surrounding the battles of Lexington and Concord are described so they can actually be felt and therefore better understood. Furthermore, as Johnny interacts with the historic Paul Revere, Dr. Warren, John Hancock, and Sam Adams, they, too, come alive with all their excitement, sadness, frustration, and passion.

In addition, Forbes's knowledge of Boston in pre-Revolutionary days helps the reader see the day-to-day life of another time. Her opening page, for example, describes the coming of day to Hancock Wharf:

> Boston slowly opened its eyes, stretched, and woke. The sun struck in horizontally from the east, flashing upon weathervanes . . . and the bells in the steeples cling-clanged, telling the people it was time to be up and about.
>
> In hundreds of houses sleepy women woke sleepier children. Get up and to work. Ephraim, get to the pump, fetch Mother water. Ann, get to the barn, milk the cow and drive her to the Common. Start the fire, Silas. Put on a clean shirt, James. Dolly, if you aren't up before I count ten. . . .[86]

It is easy for the reader to see how different life was just by seeing the various chores young people had to do two hundred years ago. But there is more to historical fiction than describing the past. Good historical fiction is also timeless. It is concerned with the universality of human behavior. Times may change, but human character remains the same. Levstik writes, "Through historical fiction, children learn that people in all times have faced change and crisis, that people in all times have basic needs in

In Johnny Tremain, *real events, like the Battle of Lexington, are described so well that they come alive for the reader.*

common, and that these needs remain in our time."[87] Thus, chores may change, but young people still have to be prodded to get out of bed. Pumpkin may be a British soldier longing for a piece of land, but anyone in any age can understand his wish to have a place to call his own. Johnny may be a boy of the eighteenth century, but his feelings of pride, hurt, doubt, confusion, and growth are felt by teenagers in any generation.

Some Critical Views

Despite the realism of its main character and its historical details, *Johnny Tremain* has been criticized by some recent critics for oversimplifying the Revolution and presenting a one-sided view. Levstik, for example, writes about objectivity and subjectivity. Whereas textbooks try to be objective in presenting facts, she says, historical fiction is subjective, that is, it presents an event through the eyes of one or more characters. Readers are permitted and sometimes influenced to make judgments about events and their morality.

Levstik maintains, however, that there are different forms of subjectivity, and she believes one can be subjective and still show different points of view. It is here that she faults *Johnny Tremain*. Although conceding its literary merits, she believes the book fails to give readers a chance to "enter the heart or mind of, say, a sympathetic loyalist or to wrestle with the moral dilemma of loyalty during a revolutionary period."[88] This leads, she believes, to a simplistic view of historic events and leaves out whole groups of people who also lived at the time. Levstik points to another book of the Revolution, *My Brother Sam Is Dead*, as an example of a book that challenges its readers more and forces them to consider hard choices.

Written by brothers James Lincoln Collier and Christopher Collier, *My Brother Sam Is Dead* is told through the eyes of a young Connecticut boy named Tim, who has a Loyalist father and Patriot brother. He sees atrocities committed on both sides. In the end, his father, even though a Loyalist, dies on a British prison ship, and his brother, a Patriot, is hanged by his own army for a crime he didn't commit. In the Afterword, Tim, now an old man telling the story, looks back and wonders if there couldn't have been a better way other than war to settle the dispute with England. Unlike *Johnny Tremain*, where the reader comes to believe in the Revolution along with Johnny, *My Brother Sam Is Dead* leads the reader to see that there are usually two sides to consider—even in a revolution.

"That a Man Can Stand Up"

Esther Forbes, however, did not believe it was possible to be neutral, to see two sides, in wartime. She said that before World War II began, she had begun research for a book about a man who remains neutral during the Revolutionary War. Then the Nazis attacked Poland, and she decided that the idea of such neutrality was absurd. Instead, she used her research to write a biography of Paul Revere and, following that, *Johnny Tremain*.

When she wrote *Johnny Tremain*, Forbes wanted her readers to see parallels between the American Revolution and World War II. Both the Patriots in 1775 and the Allies in 1943 were fighting for basic human rights. The rightness of this cause forms the core theme of *Johnny Tremain*, the thread that holds everything together and makes all sacrifices worthwhile.

Forbes presents this theme through the character of James Otis, half-mad at times because of a blow to his head. But in 1775 he is still a commanding speaker, and he comes to the last Observers meeting to deliver a powerful speech. He asks what they will fight for, listens to their answers, and proceeds to give his own. Forbes even has him foreshadow revolutions to come:

You were right, you tall, dark boy [Rab], for even as we shoot down the British soldiers we are fighting for rights such as they will be enjoying a hundred years from now.

. . . There shall be no more tyranny. A handful of men cannot seize power over thousands. A man shall choose who it is shall rule over him.

. . . The peasants of France, the serfs of Russia. Hardly more than animals now. But because we fight, they shall see freedom like a new sun rising in the west. Those natural rights God has given to every man, no matter how humble.[89]

Otis goes on to say that their generation is lucky, for not every age has a cause worth dying for.

Fighting for basic human rights is a core theme in Johnny Tremain *and is presented by James Otis through his speech to the Observers.*

Dr. Warren says good-bye to his wife. His contribution to the cause was the ultimate sacrifice.

He looks around at the Observers and predicts what each might have to sacrifice in the event of war. To wealthy John Hancock, he talks of property; to Paul Revere, he mentions his silver craft; to John Adams, he speaks of his law practice; and to Dr. Warren, he talks of hard times for the man's family should the doctor be killed in the war. All people, he says, shall give according to their abilities. Then he looks directly at Rab and predicts his death. "Some," he says, "some will give their lives. All the years of their maturity. All the children they will never live to have. The serenity of old age. To die so young is more than merely dying; it is to lose so large a part of life."[90]

Rab looks back at Otis. It seems that Rab is about to say something, but he doesn't. Otis continues his impassioned speech, finally standing up so that his head is "close against the rafters that cut down into the attic." He puts out his arms. "It is all so much simpler than you think," he says to the assembled men. He lifts his hands, pushes against the rafters, and concludes, "We give all we have, lives, property, safety, skills . . . we fight, we die, for a simple thing. Only that a man can stand up."[91]

This speech captures the central theme of the novel. Johnny is moved by Otis's words and remembers them as the fighting begins. While waiting for a chance to slip across the river, for example, he observes how differently the wounded officers and privates are treated. When an officer strikes a wounded soldier who is screaming, Johnny thinks, "It is just as James Otis said. We are fighting, partly, for just that. Because a man is a private is no reason he should be treated like cordwood."[92]

Still later, when he learns that Rab is dying, he is able to take comfort in the realization that Rab's death had meaning, that he died fighting for something right and true. Dr. Warren echoes his thoughts: "And some of us would die—so other men can stand up on their feet like men. A great many are going to die for that. They have in the past. They will a hundred years from now—two hundred. God grant there will always be men good enough. Men like Rab."[93]

As Smedman notes, *Johnny Tremain* keeps alive the belief that the American Revolution established inalienable rights for people that, if allowed to flourish, would protect mankind from tyranny, then and in the future. Otis, Johnny, Rab, Dr. Warren—they all speak for Esther Forbes's belief that those rights are still worth defending and even dying for, an important idea for young people who might be called on to lose their lives in World War II.

Collier Presents Another View

Christopher Collier, coauthor of *My Brother Sam Is Dead*, disagrees with Forbes's interpretation of the American Revolution, and therefore sees her theme as one-sided and simplistic. He compares his own novel with *Johnny Tremain* in an essay for the April 1976 issue of *Horn Book*, "Johnny and Sam: Old and New Approaches to the American Revolution." Collier believes that all written history is based on interpretation and that historical novelists present their own view of history, consciously or not. He sees *Johnny Tremain* as expressing a nineteenth-century view of the American Revolution called the Whig interpretation. This view holds that the war was fought by "freedom-loving farmers marching in a crusade to fulfill God's plan for a rationally ordered society based on principles of liberty and equality."[94] Forbes presents this view forcefully, he maintains, with James Otis as her spokesman.

While not faulting Forbes's knowledge of historic facts, Collier believes her view of the Revolution leaves out other, equally valid, interpretations. The Progressive view, for example, which holds that economics, not idealism, was the real cause of the Revolution, is quickly dismissed by Otis.

In the end, Collier says, Forbes's "presentation of the American Revolution does not pass muster as serious, professional history. Not so much because it is so sharply biased, but because it is so simplistic. Life is not like that—and we may be sure it was not like that two hundred years ago. [The American Revolution, with all of its implications for the world] is bound to be a complex matter." Collier contrasts this with his own book, in which the complexity of events gives teenagers "some raw reality to chew on."[95]

Not everyone agrees with Collier. Smedman states that Collier oversimplifies *Johnny Tremain* by focusing only on its Whig view of the Revolution and ignoring Forbes's artistic aim to "portray human greatness . . . [as] the very core of historical authenticity." Forbes wanted to show that people could rise to greatness in time of crisis, that they would fight and even die for human freedom and dignity. Perhaps the ideal of human rights expressed in the book is not realistic, given mankind's history, but Smedman says, "Even if never achieved in the future, it is a worthy goal for humans to strive after."[96]

Smedman also takes issue with Collier's charge that *Johnny Tremain* is too one-sided. Although everything is seen through Johnny's eyes—and he is definitely a Patriot—he does become friends with Lieutenant Stranger and Pumpkin, and he admires Madge's Sergeant Gale. Forbes presents each of them as real people whom Johnny finds it impossible to label as "enemies." Johnny feels sympathy for the Tory being beaten and thinks highly of Mrs. Bessie, a Patriot, when he learns that she warned the Lytes of the coming attack by the Sons of Liberty. Forbes also has Otis comment on the lack of harshness in the British occupation. She notes that the flames of liberty were lighted in Britain and that the colonists were originally demanding the rights of Englishmen. Near the end, Johnny almost takes off his hat to the British flag, not doing so only when he realizes that it is too late. The war has begun. For Johnny and Forbes, war is the right course. But she has tried to show that the British are not evil, nor are the Patriots all noble.

Two Views of War

Perhaps the differences between Forbes and Collier can best be understood by comparing their views of war and the times in which they wrote. Forbes wrote *Johnny Tremain* during a popular war with a clear enemy and defined goals. She said that once the United States entered World War II, she could no longer imagine anyone being

Johnny almost takes his hat off at the passing of the British flag.

neutral. Thus, Johnny becomes a Patriot, and although the Tories might not be evil, neither are they truly understood.

On the other hand, Christopher Collier and his brother wrote *My Brother Sam Is Dead* in 1974 during the unpopular Vietnam War. Unlike World War II, the Vietnam War drew widespread opposition and its goals were never clear. Television brought the horrors of war into people's homes, and sentiment throughout the country became more and more antiwar. In writing their novel, the Collier brothers reflected this antiwar sentiment. As Marilyn Apseloff writes in the *Illinois English Bulletin*, "The plot of *My Brother Sam Is Dead* is carefully constructed to show both sides, but more than that, as episode piles on episode, the anti-war theme emerges."[97] Forbes and her generation saw no solution other than war; Collier and his believed there could be a better way. Apseloff says in conclusion, "The chauvinistic attitudes of the forties have given way to the skepticism of the

Unlike the American Revolution and World War II, the Vietnam War generated widespread opposition, and that skepticism is reflected in the literature of its time.

seventies—to a new stress on the value of a human life—leaving young readers with ethical questions that would not have occurred to them decades ago."[98]

Ideals for a Lifetime

All literature reflects the time in which it was written. Today's young people probably share more of Collier's skepticism than Forbes's idealism. They are less likely than the World War II generation to see war as glorious; the pictures on their television screen tell them otherwise. Nevertheless, the novel's belief in the potential greatness of each individual and its message of freedom and dignity as a right for all people are timeless. So is its challenge that at some point, people must fight—in whatever way they think best—to protect that dignity and to ensure "that a man can stand up."

Notes

Introduction: "That a Man Can Stand Up"

1. Linda Kauffman Peterson and Marilyn Leathers Solt, *Newbery and Caldecott Medal and Honor Books: An Annotated Bibliography.* Boston: G. K. Hall, 1982, p. 89.

2. Peterson and Solt, *Newbery and Caldecott Medal and Honor Books,* p. xxi.

3. Alice M. Jordan, "Esther Forbes, Newbery Winner," in Bertha Mahony Miller and Elinor Whitney Field, eds., *Newbery Medal Books: 1922–1955, with Their Authors' Acceptance Papers and Related Material Chiefly from the Horn Book Magazine.* Horn Book Papers, vol. 1. Boston: Horn Book, 1955, p. 247.

4. M. G. D., "Important People—*Johnny Tremain:* A Novel for Young and Old," *Saturday Review of Literature,* November 13, 1943, p. 44.

5. Esther Forbes, *Johnny Tremain.* A Yearling Book. New York: Bantam Doubleday Dell Books for Young Readers, 1999, p. 68. (Page numbers for quotations in this book are taken from this paperback edition.)

6. Forbes, *Johnny Tremain,* pp. 136, 233.

7. Carolyn Horovitz, "Dimensions in Time: A Critical View of Historical Fiction for Children," *Horn Book,* June 1962, p. 259.

Chapter 1: Esther Forbes: Steeped in Colonial History

8. Quoted in Lynn M. Turcotte, "Esther Forbes: Her Pen Breathed Life into America's History," *Worcester Sunday Telegram,* July 9, 1972, p. 8A.

9. Quoted in Lewis Nichols, "Talk with Esther Forbes," *New York Times Book Review,* January 31, 1954, p. 14.

10. Quoted in Margaret Erskine, *Esther Forbes.* Worcester, MA: Worcester Bicentennial Commission, 1976, p. 10.

11. Erskine, *Esther Forbes,* p. 10.

12. Quoted in Jack Bales, *Esther Forbes: A Bio-Bibliography of the Author of* Johnny Tremain. Scarecrow Author Bibliographies Series, No. 98. Lanham, MD: Scarecrow Press, 1998, p. 5.

13. Quoted in Bales, *Esther Forbes,* p. 4.

14. Quoted in Bales, *Esther Forbes,* p. 5.

15. Quoted in Robert van Gelder, "An Interview with Miss Esther Forbes," *New York Times Book Review,* June 28, 1942, p. 16.

16. Bales, *Esther Forbes*, p. 6.

17. Quoted in Bales, *Esther Forbes*, p. 6.

18. Quoted in Bales, *Esther Forbes*, pp. 19, 20.

19. Quoted in van Gelder, "An Interview with Miss Esther Forbes," p. 16.

20. Quoted in Erskine, *Esther Forbes*, p. 20.

21. Erskine, *Esther Forbes*, p. 20.

22. Erskine, *Esther Forbes*, p. 22.

23. Erskine, *Esther Forbes*, p. 22.

24. Quoted in van Gelder, "An Interview with Miss Esther Forbes," p. 16.

25. Quoted in Erskine, *Esther Forbes*, p. 22.

26. Quoted in Bales, *Esther Forbes*, p. 9.

27. Quoted in Bales, *Esther Forbes*, p. 9.

28. Quoted in Bales, *Esther Forbes*, p. 37.

29. Quoted in Nichols, "Talk with Esther Forbes," p. 14.

30. Quoted in van Gelder, "An Interview with Miss Esther Forbes," p. 16.

31. Quoted in Turcotte, "Esther Forbes," p. 8A.

32. R. L. Duffus, "The Man of the Midnight Ride: Esther Forbes's Life of Paul Revere Is a Book of Distinction," *New York Times Book Review*, June 28, 1942, p. 1.

33. Quoted in van Gelder, "An Interview with Miss Esther Forbes," pp. 2, 16.

34. Quoted in Erskine, *Esther Forbes*, p. 27.

35. Quoted in Erskine, *Esther Forbes*, p. 30.

36. Quoted in Erskine, *Esther Forbes*, p. 34.

37. "Esther Forbes, Pulitzer Winner for Revere Biography, Is Dead," *New York Times*, August 13, 1967, Section 1, p. 80.

Chapter 2: A Novel for Turbulent Times

38. Esther Forbes, "Acceptance Paper," in Miller and Field, *Newbery Medal Books: 1922–1955*, p. 254.

39. Quoted in Forbes, "Acceptance Paper," p. 249.

40. Forbes, "Acceptance Paper," p. 249.

41. Forbes, "Acceptance Paper," p. 250.

42. Forbes, "Acceptance Paper," p. 251.

43. Forbes, "Acceptance Paper," p. 252.

44. Forbes, "Acceptance Paper," p. 253.

45. Alice M. Jordan, "Esther Forbes, *Johnny Tremain*," *Horn Book*, November 1943, p. 413.

46. "*Johnny Tremain* by Esther Forbes," *New Yorker*, December 4, 1943, p. 124.

47. M. G. D., "Important People—*Johnny Tremain*," p. 44.

48. P. A. Whitney, *Book Week*, November 28, 1943, p. 4. Quoted in Mertice M. James and Dorothy Brown, eds., *The Book Review Digest: Thirty-Ninth Annual Cumulation, March 1943 to February 1944 Inclusive*. New York: H. W. Wilson, 1944, p. 273.

49. Ellen Lewis Buell, "A Story of Boston and the Revolution," *New York Times Book Review*, November 14, 1943, p. 5.

50. Jordan, "Esther Forbes, *Johnny Tremain*," p. 413.

51. Jordan, "Esther Forbes, Newbery Winner," p. 247.

Chapter 3: The Story of *Johnny Tremain*

52. Forbes, *Johnny Tremain*, p. 46.

53. Forbes, *Johnny Tremain*, p. 109.

54. Forbes, *Johnny Tremain*, p. 192.

55. Forbes, *Johnny Tremain*, p. 212.

Chapter 4: The Cast of Characters

56. Forbes, *Johnny Tremain*, pp. 36–37.

57. Forbes, *Johnny Tremain*, p. 13.

58. Forbes, *Johnny Tremain*, p. 186.

59. Forbes, *Johnny Tremain*, p. 206.

60. Forbes, *Johnny Tremain*, p. 219.

61. Forbes, *Johnny Tremain*, p. 263.

62. Forbes, *Johnny Tremain*, pp. 252–53.

63. Forbes, *Johnny Tremain*, p. 217.

64. Forbes, *Johnny Tremain*, p. 59.

Chapter 5: Critical Analysis

65. Dwight L. Burton, *Literature Study in the High Schools.* 3rd ed. New York: Holt, Rinehart, and Winston, 1970, p. 266.

66. M. Sarah Smedman, "Esther Forbes' *Johnny Tremain:* Authentic History, Classic Fiction," in Perry Nodelman, ed., *Touchstones: Reflections on the Best in Children's Literature*, vol. 1. West Lafayette, IN: Children's Literature Association, 1985, p. 84.

67. Forbes, *Johnny Tremain*, p. 36.

68. Forbes, *Johnny Tremain*, p. 109.

69. Smedman, "Esther Forbes' *Johnny Tremain*," p. 85.

70. Forbes, *Johnny Tremain*, p. 212.

71. Smedman, "Esther Forbes' *Johnny Tremain*," p. 85.

72. Forbes, *Johnny Tremain*, p. 249.

73. Elyse Trevers, "*Johnny Tremain*," in Kirk H. Beetz and Suzanne Niemeyer, eds., *Beacham's Guide to Literature for Young Adults*, vol. 2. Washington, DC: Beacham, 1989, p. 697.

74. Michael Kammen, *A Season of Youth: The American Revolution and the Historical Imagination.* Ithaca, NY: Cornell University Press, 1978, p. 206.

75. Forbes, *Johnny Tremain*, pp. 159–60.

76. Quoted in Kammen, *A Season of Youth*, p. 199.

77. Kammen, *A Season of Youth*, p. 207.

78. Forbes, *Johnny Tremain*, p. 269.

79. Quoted in Turcotte, "Esther Forbes," p. 8A.

80. Rosemary K. Coffey and Elizabeth F. Howard, *America as Story: Historical Fiction for Middle and Secondary Schools.* 2nd ed. Chicago: American Library Association, 1997, p. 30.

81. Lois R. Kuznets, "Esther Forbes," in Lina Mainiero, ed., *American Women Writers: A Critical Reference Guide from Colonial Times to the Present*, vol. 2. New York: Frederick Ungar, 1980, p. 64.

82. Smedman, "Esther Forbes' *Johnny Tremain*," p. 92.

83. Cornelia Meigs, et. al., *A Critical History of Children's Literature: A Survey of Children's Books in English from Earliest Times to the Present.* New York: Macmillan, 1953, p. 500.

84. M. G. D., "Important People—*Johnny Tremain*," p. 44.

85. C. Hugh Holman, *A Handbook to Literature*. 4th ed. Indianapolis: Bobbs-Merrill, 1980, p. 214.

86. Forbes, *Johnny Tremain*, p. 7.

87. Linda Levstik, "A Gift of Time: Children's Historical Fiction," in Janet Hickman and Bernice E. Cullinan, eds., *Children's Literature in the Classroom*. Needham Heights, MA: Christopher-Gordon, 1989, p. 138.

88. Levstik, "A Gift of Time," p. 137.

89. Forbes, *Johnny Tremain*, p. 190.

90. Forbes, *Johnny Tremain*, p. 191.

91. Forbes, *Johnny Tremain*, p. 192.

92. Forbes, *Johnny Tremain*, pp. 252–53.

93. Forbes, *Johnny Tremain*, p. 266.

94. Christopher Collier, "Johnny and Sam: Old and New Approaches to the American Revolution," *Horn Book*, April 1976, p. 133.

95. Collier, "Johnny and Sam," p. 138.

96. Smedman, "Esther Forbes' *Johnny Tremain*," p. 92.

97. Marilyn Apseloff, "*Johnny Tremain* and *My Brother Sam Is Dead*: Two Views of the American Revolution," *Illinois English Bulletin*, Spring 1978, p. 19.

98. Apseloff, "*Johnny Tremain* and *My Brother Sam Is Dead*," p. 22.

For Further Exploration

Good literature helps people learn about other times, other people, and themselves. Here are suggestions for essays that explore the ideas, insights, and themes of *Johnny Tremain*.

1. Critics agree that *Johnny Tremain* is a novel of characterization, a novel in which a teenager becomes a man. Give two positive influences on Johnny and two examples of his changing attitudes and/or behavior. How do these changes show he is growing up? *See also:* M. Sarah Smedman, "Esther Forbes' *Johnny Tremain:* Authentic History, Classic Fiction," in Perry Nodelman, ed., *Touchstones: Reflections on the Best in Children's Literature,* vol. 1. West Lafayette, IN: Children's Literature Association, 1985.

2. In what ways is Johnny different from a teenager today? In what ways is he alike? *See also:* Esther Forbes, "Acceptance Paper," in Bertha Mahony Miller and Elinor Whitney Field, eds., *Newbery Medal Books: 1922–1955, with Their Authors' Acceptance Papers and Related Material Chiefly from the Horn Book Magazine.* Horn Book Papers, vol. 1. Boston: Horn Book, 1955; Carolyn Horovitz, "Dimensions in Time: A Critical View of Historical Fiction for Children," *Horn Book,* June 1962.

3. How does Esther Forbes bring pre-Revolutionary Boston to life? Give examples from the book. *See also:* Elyse Trevers, *"Johnny Tremain,"* in Kirk H. Beetz and Suzanne Niemeyer, eds., *Beacham's Guide to Literature for Young Adults,* vol. 2. Washington, DC: Beacham, 1989; Ellen Lewis Buell, "A Story of Boston and the Revolution," *New York Times Book Review,* November 14, 1943.

4. James Otis says that the American Revolution will be fought so "that a man can stand up." What does this mean? Explain how this theme is or is not still relevant today. *See also:* Smedman, "Esther Forbes' *Johnny Tremain:* Authentic History, Classic Fiction"; Elizabeth Nesbitt, "The Test of Recollection," *Newbery Medal Books: 1922–1955;* Christopher Collier, "Johnny and Sam: Old and New Approaches to the American Revolution," *Horn Book,* April 1976.

5. Pumpkin appears in only a few pages in *Johnny Tremain,* yet he becomes a powerful symbol to Johnny. What does he symbolize and how does his death become another step in Johnny's growth? *See also:* Smedman, "Esther Forbes' *Johnny Tremain:* Authentic History, Classic Fiction"; Francis R. Gemme, *Forbes' Johnny Tremain.* Monarch Notes and Study Guides. New York: Thor, 1966.

6. Although she is definitely on the side of the Patriots in *Johnny Tremain*, Esther Forbes does try to be fair to the British. Give examples from the novel that show the British are not "all bad." What does this attempt at fairness add to the novel? *See also:* Forbes, "Acceptance Paper"; Smedman, "Esther Forbes' *Johnny Tremain:* Authentic History, Classic Fiction."

7. Esther Forbes uses the literary technique of foreshadowing in *Johnny Tremain*. Define foreshadowing and find two examples in the novel. Explain how they add tension or drama. *See also:* Gemme, *Forbes' Johnny Tremain;* Marilyn Apseloff, "*Johnny Tremain* and *My Brother Sam Is Dead:* Two Views of the American Revolution," *Illinois English Bulletin*, Spring 1978.

8. Written in 1943 during the patriotic years of World War II, *Johnny Tremain* is a product of the time in which it was written. James Lincoln Collier and Christopher Collier's 1974 novel, *My Brother Sam Is Dead*, is also a product of its time, the turbulent years of the Vietnam War. Read *My Brother Sam Is Dead* and compare its view of war with that of *Johnny Tremain*. Explain how each reflects the climate of its time. *See also:* Apseloff, "*Johnny Tremain* and *My Brother Sam Is Dead:* Two Views of the American Revolution."

9. Esther Forbes was interested in the contributions of ordinary people to great events in history. Johnny himself was described by Forbes as "a human, normal boy, not too good, occasionally mischievous and downright bad." In what ways do ordinary people in *Johnny Tremain* play important roles in the coming Revolution? *See also:* Lynn M. Turcotte, "Esther Forbes: Her Pen Breathed Life into America's History," *Worcester Sunday Telegram*, July 9, 1972; Forbes, "Acceptance Paper"; Smedman, "Esther Forbes' *Johnny Tremain:* Authentic History, Classic Fiction."

10. Many historical figures interact with the fictional characters of *Johnny Tremain*, including John Hancock, Paul Revere, Sam Adams, Dr. Church, Dr. Warren, James Otis, and Josiah Quincy. Choose one and discuss his role in the novel. Research the role of this person in the Revolution after the novel ends. *See also:* Gemme, *Forbes' Johnny Tremain;* http://infoplease.kids.lycos.com.

Appendix of Criticism

Many reviews of *Johnny Tremain* appeared when it was first published, and many articles of literary criticism have been written since then. The following excerpts are selected from reviews and articles spanning over four decades.

An Outstanding Novel of Revolutionary Days

The publication of *Johnny Tremain* gives young people an outstanding novel of Revolutionary days in Boston, and may well be counted a red-letter event in children's books. Esther Forbes has now preserved for young people's reading some of the very background of her *Paul Revere,* with its details of domestic life, its penetrating knowledge of colonial Boston, its perception of character, its artistry. She tells the story of two years in the life of a boy, apprenticed to a silversmith at Hancock's Wharf, a contemporary of Paul Revere. They were important years for Boston and for the country, they witnessed the Boston Tea Party, the closing of the Port, the Battle of Lexington. Johnny's personal story, however, holds absorbed attention throughout the book. . . . Quick-tongued Johnny is no prodigy, he plays no important role in memorable deeds, but he is a true, likable boy, growing up to manhood at sixteen, to understand, as many boys are understanding today, the meaning to all men of the Liberty for which they fight. Miss Forbes ends her rare story with a moving account of the Battle of Lexington where Johnny's best friend lays down his life.

Alice M. Jordan, *Horn Book,* November 1943.

A Person of Importance

If Jonathan Lyte Tremain never lived in the flesh, he lives vividly with the men of his time in this book. So we dare to put him among the people of importance.

He is a boy, an apprentice to a silversmith in Boston, when we meet him just before the American Revolution. Casting the handle of a sugar basin for John Hancock, he seriously burns his right hand. . . . Johnny goes through some hard and bitter times before he finds his work in the struggle that is to free the Colonies from British rule. The solution comes through a young printer, who likes Johnny and befriends him. Rab, too, is a "person of importance." His death of a mortal wound after the Battle of Lexington affects us as do the reports that are coming now from the fighting fronts. It leaves us with the feeling of futility, an agony of pity for a life that might mean so much if allowed to mature.

M. G. D., *Saturday Review of Literature,* November 13, 1943.

Revolution and Johnny Bound Together

Johnny saw in the Observer's garret, the Revolution simmer, come, under Sam Adams' shrewd hot breath, swiftly to a boil.

He smelled, one riotous night, the fragrance of "salt-water tea," he helped Paul Revere start on his ride—"one if by land and two if by sea"—saw Billy Dawes start merrily off disguised as a drunken farmer. He saw Yankee Doodle coming to town, blood in his eye and honest rage in his heart, and, if he wasn't on hand for the shot fired round the world, he heard and never forgot half-mad James Otis' impassioned words: "We give all we have, lives, property, safety, skills . . . we fight, we die for a simple thing. Only that a man can stand up."

Thus Johnny became a man and an American. The proportion between his personal fortunes and the larger theme of the Revolution is so delicately balanced that never for a moment does one forget either. The one is part and parcel of the other, true test of the novelist's skill.

Ellen Lewis Buell, "A Story of Boston and the Revolution,"
New York Times Book Review, November 14, 1943.

Not Serious, Professional History

Johnny Tremain, with its message of ideologically motivated war, is so much the product of World War II that one who grew up in the 1940's must honor its clear one-sidedness. Younger historians . . . would be less tolerant. But without denying its outstanding literary merit, Miss Forbes' presentation of the American Revolution does not pass muster as serious, professional history. Not so much because it is so sharply biased, but because it is so simplistic. Life is not like that—and we may be sure it was not like that two hundred years ago. Such an event as a war involving the three major European nations, with implications for the western power structure for centuries to come, is bound to be a complex matter. To present history in simple, one-sided—almost moralistic—terms, is to teach nothing worth learning and to falsify the past in a way that provides worse than no help in understanding the present or in meeting the future.

Christopher Collier, "Johnny and Sam:
Old and New Approaches to the American
Revolution," *Horn Book*, April 1976.

Making the Revolution Real

To many students, even after considerable exposure to American history, the American Revolution remains a rather remote and hazy melange of tea in Boston Harbor, a midnight ride of Paul Revere, and patriots whose feet were frozen at Valley Forge. A novel like Esther Forbes's *Johnny Tremain* provides a moving close-up of that momentous time from the point of view of a realistic adolescent; [an] understanding of the time and its issues as they entered the lives of people, which no history text can supply, is apparent in the imaginative work. . . . Out of her research on the pre-Revolutionary War years, the author, who won a Pulitzer Prize for her biography of Paul Revere, has wrought the authentic background for her story of a young Boston silversmith's apprentice who became involved in patriotic activities . . . just prior to the outbreak of hostilities. Famous figures such as Paul Revere and Samuel Adams play important parts in the story. . . . Johnny's personal tribulations are the major subject of the story, but the adolescent reader is able to live with Johnny through the stirring pre–Bunker Hill times in a manner that marks the best in historical fiction.

> Dwight L. Burton, *Literature Study in the High Schools.* 3rd ed. New York: Holt, Rinehart, and Winston, 1970.

Johnny as a Symbol of the Revolution

The character Johnny, proud but ultimately tolerant of others' faults and points of view, flawed but at last courageous enough to take measures to compensate for his deficiencies, to heal his wounds, down-to-earth but sufficiently idealistic to believe that individual human freedom and dignity is worth fighting for, is symbolic of Revolutionary Boston as portrayed by Forbes. *Johnny Tremain* keeps alive the American myth that, in Leonard Wibberly's words, ["]our Revolution established certain inalienable rights for people, which if preserved would protect mankind from tyranny in all the centuries ahead." That ideal may be irreconcilable with conditions wrought by mankind in the past and in the present. Even if never achieved in the future, it is a worthy goal for humans to strive for.

> M. Sarah Smedman, "Esther Forbes' *Johnny Tremain:* Authentic History, Classic Fiction," in Perry Nodelman, ed., *Touchstones: Reflections on the Best in Children's Literature*, vol. 1. West Lafayette, IN: Children's Literature Association, 1985.

Johnny as a Normal Boy

It is easy for the reader to identify himself with Johnny; he has so many faults but is at the same time so lovable. He could have been a friend to miserable, lonesome Dove, but he bullied him, and few children could forgive Johnny had he been otherwise. He made promises to Cilla, but failed her often; he was both deeply loyal to Rab and jealous of him. His tongue was too quick and his courage often failed him, but the core of his being was strong and idealistic, and it took only Rab's unspoken faith in him to tip the scale on the right side, making it possible for him to accept the bitterness of his first great defeat as a challenge and a new beginning.

> Cornelia Meigs et al., *A Critical History of Children's Literature: A Survey of Children's Books in English from Earliest Times to the Present.* Chapter Two: "Adventures in the Past." New York: Macmillan, 1953.

Two Views of War

More important than side-taking in *Johnny Tremain* is the idea that war can be glorious. The character who stated that he considered himself lucky . . . for having a cause worth dying for adds: "This honor is not given to every generation." Obviously, Esther Forbes was reflecting a sentiment prevalent during World War II. She wrote from the point of view of the forties when she has a character say: "Some of us (will) die—so other men can stand up on their feet like men. A great many are going to die for that. They have in the past. They will a hundred years from now—two hundred. God grant there will always be men good enough." The Collier brothers also realized that men have fought for hundreds of years, but from their perspective of the seventies, fighting no longer seems to be the wonderful solution it had been. For them, somehow there must be a better way. Their attitude is reflected in *My Brother Sam Is Dead*.

> Marilyn Apseloff, "*Johnny Tremain* and *My Brother Sam Is Dead:* Two Views of the American Revolution," *Illinois English Bulletin*, Spring 1978.

The American Revolution as a Rite of Passage

Johnny Tremain is offered as a personalization of Revolutionary Boston and its inevitable destiny. . . . Its plot, quite simply, is an epitome of the American Revolution as *rite de passage* . . . [and the book] encapsulates the dominant view of our Revolution in American popular culture. . . .

Johnny's time of troubles and his symbolic rebirth coincide exactly with that of the colonies. The winter of 1773–4 is pivotal. As the pretty Cilla says to Johnny: "This is the end. The end of one thing—the beginning of something else . . . there is going to be a war—civil war." . . . At the end Miss Forbes refers more and more to manhood, not merely Johnny's achieving it, but his passing through a crisis of confidence about courage, manliness, and even the acceptance of death in a just cause. The book's last words, "A man can stand up," provide a residual refrain throughout.

The fact that Johnny discovers his parentage and true identity in 1775, at the age of sixteen, is quite obviously symbolic though not nearly so heavy-handed as my flat statement of it might sound. Likewise the fact that his tragic injury forces him to rethink his calling. And likewise the fact that all these personal troubles . . . have served to prepare him for Lexington, Concord, Independence, and a brave new world beyond that. He has undergone the psychic experience required to transform a boorish, socially inferior adolescent provincial into a militant, morally superior young American.

Michael Kammen, *A Season of Youth: The American*
Revolution and the Historical Imagination.
Chapter Six: "The American Revolution as
National *Rite de Passage.*" Ithaca, NY:
Cornell University Press, 1978.

Pumpkin as a Symbol of the British Soldier

Pumpkin symbolizes the professional British soldier and is characteristic of those stationed in the colonies at that time. Trained as a soldier, he says he will fight if it becomes necessary, but his sympathies are with the colonists. In America he sees . . . an opportunity to own his own land and become a farmer in his own right. The possibility of this in England had been severely limited for decades because of the small land area and the large population; also, what land was available was owned by a few large landholders.

Pumpkin's desire for this is so great that he decides to desert, and with the aid of Johnny, he does so. Caught a short time later, he is shot for desertion.

Francis R. Gemme, *Forbes' Johnny Tremain.*
Monarch Notes and Study Guides.
New York: Thor, 1966.

Understated Style

Forbes' technique of conveying strong feeling through description of exterior behavior typifies her preferences for understatement, and serves to soften harsh reality, to avoid sentimentality, and to heighten genuine emotion. Her style creates a tension between subject matter and the language restraining it. When Rab is dying, all we are told about Johnny is that he "walked disconsolately about the chamber. He looked out the window. He picked up a pewter candlestick and examined the maker's mark." When Rab called to him, "Johnny went to him, sat on the floor beside his chair and put his hands over Rab's thin ones." Johnny's inexpressible feelings echo through the simple, staccato sentences and the fragments in which he responds to Rab: "'I'll take good care of it.' . . . 'Anything.' . . . 'I'll go.'"

> M. Sarah Smedman, "Esther Forbes' *Johnny Tremain:* Authentic
> History, Classic Fiction," in Perry Nodelman, ed., *Touchstones: Re-*
> *flections on the Best in Children's Literature*, vol. 1. West Lafayette,
> IN: Children's Literature Association, 1985.

Importance of the Individual

Johnny Tremain is the briefer, focused, and fictionalized outgrowth of *Paul Revere and the World He Lived In.* . . . Both the life of the real silversmith and the now-famous story of the silversmith's apprentice who adjusts to the handicap of a maimed hand and participates in the Boston revolutionary movement, display [Forbes's] intense interest in the part that individuals, significant or insignificant, play in historical events. Both books clearly owe their immediate inspiration to [Forbes's] concern with the meaning and nature of human freedom in the context of World War II.

> Lois R. Kuznets, "Esther Forbes," in Lina Mainiero, ed., *American*
> *Women Writers: A Critical Reference Guide from Colonial Times*
> *to the Present*, vol. 2. New York: Frederick Ungar, 1980.

Timeline of Events in *Johnny Tremain*

Historical Events

1773
British Parliament passes Tea Act, retains tax on tea, gives East India Tea Company exclusive rights to sell tea in colonies. Colonists call for tax repeal.

December 1773
Boston Tea Party destroys tea shipment.

June 1774
Britain closes the port of Boston; more troops arrive, tensions mount.

Fall 1774
First Continental Congress meets in Philadelphia.

April 1775
Battles of Lexington and Concord.

Events in *Johnny Tremain*

Summer 1773
Hancock orders sugar bowl; Johnny burns his hand.

September 1773
Johnny meets Rab, is tried for theft of silver cup, begins work at the *Boston Observer*.

December 1773
Johnny participates in Boston Tea Party.

June 1774
Johnny works at Afric Queen, where British officers are quartered.

August 1774
Lyte family attacked by Sons of Liberty at summer home in Milton.

Fall 1774
Last Observers meeting; James Otis delivers "that a man can stand up" speech; Sam Adams and John Adams prepare to attend First Continental Congress.

Fall 1774–Spring 1775
Johnny becomes part of Paul Revere's spy network, befriends Dove to obtain information.

April 1775
Pumpkin is executed for desertion; Rab leaves to join Minutemen in Lexington; Johnny delivers news of impending British march to Dr. Warren. Rab fatally wounded at Lexington; Johnny consents to have Dr. Warren operate on his hand, determined to join the fight for a new country.

Chronology of Events in Esther Forbes's Life

1891
Esther Forbes is born in Westboro, Massachusetts, on June 28.

1898
Family moves to nearby Worcester.

1900
Contracts rheumatic fever, which permanently damages her heart; long weeks in bed help develop her creative talents.

1903
Starts first novel, *Patroclus*, about Greek hero Achilles and the fall of Troy.

1912
Graduates from Bradford Academy, junior college in Bradford, Massachusetts.

1915
Accompanies her sister Katharine to University of Wisconsin and takes courses.

1916
Short story, "Break-Neck Hill," published by *Wisconsin Literary Magazine*, later included in *O. Henry Memorial Award Prize Stories of 1920*.

1917
United States enters World War I; Forbes joins the war effort by volunteering to work on West Virginia farm; returns for two more summers.

1919
Returns home to Boston; begins working for publisher Houghton Mifflin as a reader of unsolicited manuscripts.

1926
Marries Albert Hoskins, a graduate of Harvard Law School, and moves with him to New York; Houghton Mifflin publishes *O Genteel Lady!*; novel receives favorable reviews, becomes a best-seller.

1928
A Mirror for Witches published; like first novel, receives excellent reviews; Forbes and Hoskins move back to Boston.

1929
Stock market crash; Great Depression begins.

1933
Forbes and Hoskins divorce; Forbes moves back to family home in Worcester.

1935
Miss Marvel published.

1937
Paradise published.

1938
The General's Lady published.

1939
Hitler invades Poland; World War II begins in Europe.

1941
Japanese attack Pearl Harbor on December 7; United States declares war on Japan and enters the war against Hitler in Europe.

1942
Biography *Paul Revere and the World He Lived In* published.

1943
Paul Revere and the World He Lived In receives Pulitzer Prize in history; *Johnny Tremain* published.

1944
Johnny Tremain wins prestigious Newbery Award for excellence in children's literature.

1945
World War II ends; Germany surrenders on May 7; Japan agrees to surrender August 14, after the United States drops atomic bombs on Hiroshima and Nagasaki on August 6 and 9.

1946
Children's biography *America's Paul Revere* published.

1947
The Boston Book, a pictorial essay, published in collaboration with photographer Arthur Griffin.

1948
The Running of the Tide published, wins the MGM prize for best novel of the year.

1951
Forbes's mother dies at the age of ninety-five.

1954
Rainbow on the Road, her last novel, published.

1956
Begins work on favorite project, the history of witchcraft in seventeenth-century Massachusetts.

1957
Disney releases film version of *Johnny Tremain*.

1960
Becomes the first woman elected to the American Antiquarian Society in Worcester.

1967
Dies of rheumatic heart disease on August 12.

Works Consulted

Major Editions of *Johnny Tremain*

Esther Forbes, *Johnny Tremain: A Novel for Old and Young.* Boston: Houghton Mifflin, 1943.

Johnny Tremain: A Novel for Old and Young. Student's Edition. Boston: Houghton Mifflin, 1945. (Contains an introduction by Forbes in which she provides historical and cultural background to the story, as well as her philosophy that, although times change, the essence of human nature does not change.)

Esther Forbes, *Johnny Tremain.* A Yearling Book. New York: Bantam Doubleday Dell, 1987.

Esther Forbes, *Johnny Tremain: A Novel for Old and Young.* Audio-Cassette. Blackstone Audio Books, 1994.

Esther Forbes, *Johnny Tremain.* Illustrated American Classics. Illustrated by Michael McCurdy. Boston: Houghton Mifflin, 1998.

Esther Forbes, *Johnny Tremain.* A Yearling Book. New York: Bantam Doubleday Dell Books for Young Readers, 1999. Page numbers for quotations in this book are taken from this edition.

Also by Esther Forbes

Paul Revere and the World He Lived In. Boston: Houghton Mifflin, 1942. Comprehensive biography of Paul Revere, winner of the 1943 Pulitzer Prize in history.

America's Paul Revere. Boston: Houghton Mifflin, 1946. Illustrated biography for young people.

"Acceptance Paper," in Bertha Mahony Miller and Elinor Whitney Field, eds., *Newbery Medal Books: 1922–1955, with Their Authors' Acceptance Papers and Related Material Chiefly from the Horn Book Magazine.* Horn Book Papers, vol. 1. Boston: Horn Book, 1955. Delivered on receiving the Newbery Award, this paper discusses how Forbes came to write *Johnny Tremain* and her belief that the young people of her time were facing similar challenges.

About Esther Forbes

Jack Bales, *Esther Forbes: A Bio-Bibliography of the Author of* Johnny Tremain. Scarecrow Author Bibliographies Series, No. 98. Lanham, MD: Scarecrow Press, 1998. Contains a brief but comprehensive biography, Forbes's acceptance speech for the Newbery Award, and an annotated bibliography with excerpts from criticism of all of Forbes's work.

Margaret Erskine, *Esther Forbes.* Worcester, MA: Worcester Bicentennial Commission, 1976. Written by the wife of Forbes's nephew, this short book traces Forbes's life from early childhood and gives insights into her strong family ties.

"Esther Forbes, Pulitzer Winner for Revere Biography, Is Dead," *New York Times,* August 13, 1967. Obituary giving highlights of her life and work calls her "a novelist who wrote like a historian and a historian who wrote like a novelist."

Lewis Nichols, "Talk with Esther Forbes," *New York Times Book Review,* January 31, 1954. Contains quotations relating to Forbes's early interest in historical writing and her mature writing habits.

Lynn M. Turcotte, "Esther Forbes: Her Pen Breathed Life into America's History," *Worcester Sunday Telegram,* July 9, 1972. This hometown newspaper article uses many direct quotations from Forbes in its summary of her life.

Robert van Gelder, "An Interview with Miss Esther Forbes," *New York Times Book Review,* June 28, 1942. Forbes tells about her early writings and how she came to write her Pulitzer Prize–winning biography of Paul Revere.

Literary Criticism

Marilyn Apseloff, "*Johnny Tremain* and *My Brother Sam Is Dead:* Two Views of the American Revolution," *Illinois English Bulletin,* Spring 1978. Discusses the two novels' views of the Revolution in terms of when they were written and shows how each novel is a product of its time.

Ellen Lewis Buell, "A Story of Boston and the Revolution," *New York Times Book Review,* November 14, 1943. Relates important events in the book and praises Forbes's skill as both a novelist and historian.

Dwight L. Burton, *Literature Study in the High Schools.* 3rd ed. New York: Holt, Rinehart, and Winston, 1970. Discusses the importance of literature in secondary curricula. In a section called "Varieties of the Junior Novel," discusses historical fiction as a vehicle for expressing truths about human nature and uses *Johnny Tremain* as an outstanding example of the genre for young people.

Rosemary K. Coffey and Elizabeth F. Howard, *America as Story: Historical Fiction for Middle and Secondary Schools.* 2nd ed. Chicago: American Library Association, 1997. Briefly discusses more than a hundred historical novels that deal with American history. Gives brief plot summary and says *Johnny Tremain* allows readers to see everyday lives of people in his time.

Christopher Collier, "Johnny and Sam: Old and New Approaches to the American Revolution," *Horn Book*, April 1976. Explains *Johnny Tremain*'s Whig view of the American Revolution, discusses other views, and then calls the novel simplistic and one-sided. He also briefly contrasts *Johnny Tremain* with his own book, *My Brother Sam Is Dead*.

M. G. D., "Important People—*Johnny Tremain: A Novel for Young and Old*," *Saturday Review of Literature*, November 13, 1943. Favorable review praising the details, characters, and "aliveness" of the book. Calls Johnny Tremain an "important person" because he "lives" with the people of his time.

R. L. Duffus, "The Man of the Midnight Ride: Esther Forbes's Life of Paul Revere Is a Book of Distinction," *New York Times Book Review*, June 28, 1942. Review of Paul Revere biography praising Forbes's knowledge of the time and discussing Revere's many accomplishments besides the "midnight ride."

Francis R. Gemme, *Forbes' Johnny Tremain*. Monarch Notes and Study Guides. New York: Thor, 1966. A study guide to the book, including plot, characters, themes, and literary techniques.

C. Hugh Holman, *A Handbook to Literature*. 4th ed. Indianapolis: Bobbs-Merrill, 1980. Presents definitions, in alphabetical order, of literary terms used in discussing British and American literature.

Carolyn Horovitz, "Dimensions in Time: A Critical View of Historical Fiction for Children," *Horn Book*, June 1962. Discusses the concept of time in historical fiction and how the story relates to the period of history that serves as its setting. Horovitz sees *Johnny Tremain* as an excellent example of a character and story so much a part of their time period that reading about Johnny "becomes reading about the American Revolution."

"*Johnny Tremain* by Esther Forbes," *New Yorker*, December 4, 1943. Brief review emphasizing historic insights.

Alice M. Jordan, "Esther Forbes, *Johnny Tremain*," *Horn Book*, November 1943. Brief favorable review praising the book for its details of colonial life and its understanding of character. Notes the relationship between the colonists' struggle and World War II.

———, "Esther Forbes, Newbery Winner," in Bertha Mahony Miller and Elinor Whitney Field, eds., *Newbery Medal Books: 1922–1955, with Their Authors' Acceptance Papers and Related Material Chiefly from the Horn Book Magazine*. Horn Book Papers, vol. 1. Boston: Horn Book, 1955. Brief biographical essay giving highlights of Forbes's life, especially her New England background.

Discusses her fascination with the "whys" of human behavior and her skill in writing historical novels.

Michael Kammen, *A Season of Youth: The American Revolution and the Historical Imagination*. Ithaca, NY: Cornell University Press, 1978. A somewhat advanced book discussing the role of the American Revolution in popular national tradition and how history's view of the Revolution changes as the country and culture change. *Johnny Tremain* appears in chapter 6, in which Kammen discusses and criticizes the "rite of passage" view of the Revolution.

Lois R. Kuznets, "Esther Forbes," in Lina Mainiero, ed., *American Women Writers: A Critical Reference Guide from Colonial Times to the Present*, vol. 2. New York: Frederick Ungar, 1980. Contains brief biographical and critical discussions of women writers. Mentions Forbes's interest in the role ordinary people played in historical events.

Linda Levstik, "A Gift of Time: Children's Historical Fiction," in Janet Hickman and Bernice E. Cullinan, eds., *Children's Literature in the Classroom*. Needham Heights, MA: Christopher-Gordon, 1989. Discusses the role of historical fiction in giving young people a chance to experience the past as they identify with the joys, sorrows, and conflicts of characters who lived in other times. Criticizes *Johnny Tremain* for not giving readers a chance to enter into the minds of those opposing the Revolution.

Cornelia Meigs, et al., *A Critical History of Children's Literature: A Survey of Children's Books in English from Earliest Times to the Present*. New York: Macmillan, 1953. A reference book of children's books, discussing *Johnny Tremain* in the section called "Adventures in the Past." Praises Forbes's ability to make Johnny and Boston so real and alive.

Elizabeth Nesbitt, "The Test of Recollection," in Bertha Mahony Miller and Elinor Whitney Field, eds., *Newbery Medal Books: 1922–1955, with Their Authors' Acceptance Papers and Related Material Chiefly from the Horn Book Magazine*. Horn Book Papers, vol. 1. Boston: Horn Book, 1955. Discusses the Newbery Award and its criteria, focusing on a few books, including *Johnny Tremain*. Sees Otis's "that a man can stand up" speech as the central theme, one that not only reflects the meaning of the American Revolution, but also expresses man's long struggle for individual freedom.

Linda Kauffman Peterson and Marilyn Leathers Solt, *Newbery and Caldecott Medal and Honor Books: An Annotated Bibliography*. Boston: G. K. Hall, 1982. Gives brief history of Newbery and

Caldecott awards and a discussion of recipients. Praises *Johnny Tremain's* historical realism and the characterization of Johnny.

M. Sarah Smedman, "Esther Forbes' *Johnny Tremain:* Authentic History, Classic Fiction," in Perry Nodelman, ed., *Touchstones: Reflections on the Best in Children's Literature*, vol. 1. West Lafayette, IN: Children's Literature Association, 1985. Discusses all aspects of *Johnny Tremain:* characterization, historical realism, themes, and the excitement of the story as a way of explaining the novel's popularity through the years.

Elyse Trevers, "*Johnny Tremain*," in Kirk H. Beetz and Suzanne Niemeyer, eds., *Beacham's Guide to Literature for Young Adults*, vol. 2. Washington, DC: Beacham, 1989. Contains essays about works of fiction and biography for young people. The six-page section on *Johnny Tremain* contains a brief author biography, critical analysis, questions for further thought, and a bibliography.

P. A. Whitney, *Book Week*, November 28, 1943, in Mertice M. James and Dorothy Brown, eds., *The Book Review Digest: Thirty-Ninth Annual Cumulation, March 1943 to February 1944 Inclusive*. New York: H. W. Wilson, 1944. Brief excerpt of a favorable review praising characterization and sense of history.

Index

Picture Credits

About the Author

Elizabeth Weiss Vollstadt is a freelance writer and a former teacher. She has a B.A. from Adelphi University and an M.A. from John Carroll University, both in English. She has written two books for Lucent Books Teen Issues series. Her short stories for young people, many with historic settings, have appeared in publications such as *Highlights for Children, Children's Digest, Jack and Jill, My Friend,* and *The Christian Family Christmas Book.* "I loved *Johnny Tremain* when I was in junior high," she says, "and later I also enjoyed teaching it. It's been fun to relive Johnny's experiences again." Vollstadt now lives in DeLand, Florida, with her husband, where she divides her time between writing and boating on the St. Johns River.